Secondary Drama: A Creative Source Book

What is a compelling scheme of work and how do I create one? What are the building blocks of drama? How do I sustain interest and engagement? What is the purpose and impact of my daily work?

Providing inspiration for daily practice alongside a full range of tried and tested schemes of work, this exciting new book offers support to secondary teachers wanting to create original drama experiences to meet their own unique classroom needs.

The book models a positive and reflective approach to classroom practice, offering a thoughtful exploration of the craft and art of drama teaching, covering key issues such as classroom management, student engagement, planning, progression and assessment. After considering the theory behind drama in education and the fundamentals of practice, the majority of the text is devoted to the annotated schemes of work. These cover a diverse range of topics such as homelessness, addiction, terrorism and civil rights and show how the ideas discussed can be put into practice.

Featuring a Foreword by Dorothy Heathcote and a Preface by Edward Bond, this resource will be valuable reading for both new and established teachers looking to deliver excellent, inspiring drama lessons across the secondary setting and become vibrant and effective drama specialists.

John Doona is a qualified advanced skills teacher with a wide experience of primary and secondary drama practice, a visiting lecturer in drama at the University of Chester and a professional writer; with dramatic work broadcast on Radio 4 and performed by the Royal Court Young People's Theatre and elsewhere. He is also the creator and director of the Children's Shakespeare Festivals, a series of projects now in its sixth year.

Secondary Drama: A Creative Source Book

Practical inspiration for teachers

John Doona

Routledge
Taylor & Francis Group

LONDON AND NEW YORK

Dedicated to Edward and Elizabeth Bond

First published 2014
by Routledge
2 Park Square, Milton Park, Abingdon, Oxon OX14 4RN

Simultaneously published in the USA and Canada
by Routledge
711 Third Avenue, New York, NY 10017

Routledge is an imprint of the Taylor & Francis Group, an informa business

British Library Cataloguing in Publication Data
A catalogue record for this book is available from the British Library

Library of Congress Cataloging in Publication Data
Doona, John.
Secondary drama : a creative source book : practical inspiration for teachers /
John Doona.
pages cm
1. Drama—Study and teaching (Secondary) I. Title.
PN1701.D66 2013
809.2'0071'2—dc23
2013014931

ISBN: 978-0-415-81136-1 (hbk)
ISBN: 978-0-415-81137-8 (pbk)
ISBN: 978-1-315-88463-9 (ebk)

Typeset in Helvetica
by FiSH Books Ltd, Enfield

MIX
Paper from
responsible sources
FSC
www.fsc.org   FSC® C013056

Printed and bound in Great Britain by
TJ International Ltd, Padstow, Cornwall

Contents

Foreword

Dorothy Heathcote was an original and great spirit. She moved from the factory floor to renowned professorship and along the way established much of the approach, language and working practices of the Drama-in-Education we work with today; her legacy of human and humanising educational practice remains a bulwark against reducing forms of schooling.

Dorothy wrote this introduction several years ago and in it, she gives a brief and personally charged history of an education system moving towards something much less rich than she would have hoped for. If you are a drama specialist, you are already a 'friend of Dorothy' and your daily practice is already part of the struggle for humanness and meaning.

We are grateful to her family for permission to publish the piece posthumously.

The State We're In (with apologies to Will Hutton)

A touch of history

The national curriculum came about because of anxiety, not a developed sense of what schooling is supposed to be for. It arose as governments started to worry about how our education system stands up to comparisons with other countries. This is based in economics rather than commitments to developed beliefs or recognition of how our culture is in a state of flux. One result is the plethora of schemes, advice and 'nipping and tucking' about what should be taught.

We have experts who devise dreams of excellence. These are fed to organisations in authority. These in turn arrive on the desks of administrators and eventually, with the teachers who must interpret these edicts to their students in face-to-face encounters. Along the way publishers get a grip, and this means 'expert' writers and devisers of programmes and book layouts. There's a lot of money spent there. Then there are the training days to help the teachers understand the detail of the 'curriculum delivery'.

Teaching, like driving a car and playing football, is an open skill. No two encounters with classes are ever the same. All the careful devising of curriculum text books and complete programmes can't be fulfilled if teachers have no trust in their open skills to live in the moment of mind encounters with their students. They need to plan for flexibility, base their teaching in committed belief-systems and overcome their anxieties about students being involved in group work which invites them to contribute their own ideas and matters of concern, which is the basis of humanised schooling. This entails developing strategies for awakening students' social sense and involving them in exploring circumstances and contexts which have *relevance* and which use school time to learn that which will serve them throughout their lives.

Many factors make this hazardous. The environmental arrangements cannot be said in the main to be imaginative or stimulating. The provision in many schools serves little more than the basic means of writing, reading, listening, watching and hopefully, holding interesting discourse. Then there is time-clock time – divided to ensure that all have fair access to curriculum subject areas based on content-driven information. This implies subject teachers who 'know their stuff', and presumes that they are passionate to share that knowledge. No other establishment in our culture uses the kind of talk which teachers and students indulge in during class encounters. When released from this 'clock-content-corset' teachers and students re-assume their contextual and cultural existence when the school day is over.

There is noone to blame. Historically, schools were devised so that all could learn to calculate, read and write, and make communication and fraternisation more efficient and satisfying. For a time, right up to my mother's schooling, this was embraced as 'a good thing'. Even then it didn't suit everybody. Family priorities caused absences – potato picking, farm jobs, child-minding, washday, helping out – with sons and daughters hauled in to help. School was never the sole means of learning.

Then the subject areas were divided as travel possibilities developed and knowledge of history started to matter. Two great wars brought about shifts in cultural attitudes and expectations. The division between academic and craft courses became established. However, the school system continued to operate on content-based experiences; more so in the academic schemes. Craft courses, at least, enabled teachers and learners to operate their encounters through tools, which by their nature impose disciplines and opportunities for skill development.

When the anxiety about standards gripped the government these courses were in the main axed in favour of the earliest subjects of numeracy and aspects of communication. So we saw the down-grading of woodwork, cookery, laundry (sic), metalwork, music and aspects of arts and physical activity, and with them went teachers whose classrooms were active and often individualised. Anxiety caused emphasis on testing for progression, and further, reinforced a content-driven curriculum because that is open to scrutiny and the awarding of marks.

Given the addiction to tests and the time driven organisation of tasks, what hope is there for change? To move from *content* teaching to *contextual* learning requires a curriculum based in humanising the strategies for classroom encounters. Dramatic work permits this change because it involves people in context-driven learning. It is a social art based on co-operation between individuals and is about matters of human concern. One face of dramatic learning relates to theatre devising. There are many other forms which can be used in humanising the curriculum currently deemed essential. The main change will involve teachers and learners in devising human contexts. This does not mean dispensing with all the other ways of learning – research, subject-skills, lectures and presentations. Human contexts mean making contracts that students and teachers will engage with now, in immediate time, as they work from within the boundaries of people involved with sorting out a problem, or question attitudes or examine forces operating in historical contexts.

The umbrella of drama permits social outcomes to be considered, questioned, and alternative resolutions to be explored. Drama is always based (whatever the subject) on contained and disciplined human encounters and precise concerns. It is a shape-shifter spanning all periods, social divisions, cultural pressures and human content expressed via *contexts*.

You can't test for the social health of students. You can't test for shifts in imagination, co-operation and accommodation with and towards others. You can't test for risk-taking in teachers and students. Above all, you can't award points to teachers and students for their individual capacities to develop empathy, enthusiasm for learning, self-discipline and commitment to keep on learning. Shakespeare's 'mirror up to nature' stills holds, and is the very devil to asses, judge and reward by a scale of marks.

In the shape-shifting sands of using humanised contexts through drama, each teacher has perforce to use a blend of personal belief and standards, style and scope of strategies, vision and intuition and risk, in creating productive learning encounters with classes. This means shrugging off the 'black dog' of fear and anxiety recorded as early as 1577. The 'Black Shuck' haunts us all and appears more frequently as society brings changes in pupil behaviour and teachers face challenges all the more direct because content situations no longer fill their students needs in a climate where they refuse to shed contextually lived lives at the school portals.

John Doona is a teacher who has responded to these challenges and this book reflects his passionate commitment to involving his students in co-operative, imaginative, culturally-disciplined, focused work related to their lives and concerns. Each chapter reveals the move to make his beliefs work in the day-to-day contacts with his students. You don't have to agree with everything he writes and does in his classroom. He invites you to enter and give it some consideration, especially, to use it to extend or review your own thinking and recognise your own drives and aspirations. All books, like all arts, read us, as we encounter the ideas they hold.

Dorothy Heathcote

Preface

If Dorothy Heathcote is the great spirit of the educationally centred drama world, then perhaps her lost sibling in a wider theatre context is master playwright, Edward Bond. In a similar fashion, Bond has devoted his life to working for a humanising drama. Bond's plays and his aesthetic framework might be seen as 'the other half of the sky' to drama-in-education; it helps us to understand our work and to build a sense of purpose.

We hope that his introduction will begin to prise the lid off established patterns of thought and stimulate an open and struggling spirit of enquiry that lets us imagine beyond the hard horizon.

A poor man longed to be rich. Halfway through his life he unexpectedly inherited a great fortune. Of course, he spent it on expensive rubbish he did not need. His new mansions were Aladdin's caves crammed with junk. He became addicted to anything that could be consumed: drugs, alcohol, gadgets, speed – and the paranoia, anger and envy that were consuming *him*. He was possessed by his possessions. It was as if he had caught a disease. His life became a fast-track journey to its end and a pauper's funeral, because his fortune vanished as quickly as his skin was withered away by his fevers. He died years sooner than he would have if he had not had the good luck to inherit a great fortune.

We can see ourselves in this poor man who became rich and made himself poorer. Technology has given us a world of new things which we do not know how to use without endangering our happiness and our planet. Ultimately, drama is about using these things wisely and living in a shared humanness. That's why the Greeks, who laid the foundations of modern drama, wrote tragedies. Not to remind us of the sufferings brought by want and need (they are always apparent and we do not need to be reminded of them) but to remind us that good fortune also brings dangers. It is why the Greeks drove Euripides, the most important Greek dramatist for our times, into exile. He was too truthful. If he had lived now he would not be asked to write for films or TV – and he would not do so even if he were asked. Instead the greatest of Greek dramatists would have chosen to write for young people.

Drama is not concerned with an ideal world. If we ever got to Utopia we would find it had been ruined by the people who got there before us. Drama is about the things of this world. The power of modern technology penetrates society so deeply that it begins to destroy drama and its power to further our humanness. The Greeks rewarded their dramatists with honour; Hollywood and TV reward their dramatists with money – which is why they soon begin to write for the market and not for human understanding. In our time people living under political and theocratic dictatorships struggle and die to create new democracies – and we allow our own democracy to be corrupted by TV and Hollywood. They divide imagination from reason so that imagination becomes wishful fantasy and reason becomes irrational. Their sentimentality disguises their superficiality and brutality and their pandering to intolerance and vigilantism.

Throughout history truths have been entangled with lies. The truths that enable people to live and prosper together are held only at the cost of ideological distortions. Community becomes nationalism and tribalism, religion becomes fanaticism, culture becomes deprivation and elitism. These are corruptions of imagination. Absurd beliefs elevate fictions into destructive, false realities. And as technological innovation unsettles society even more, beliefs become more fanatical and violent.

We confuse fiction, drama and reality. Theatre is fiction – it may seem to be harmless entertainment or wishful thinking, but because it avoids responsibility for human reality, for the way we really think and live, it fosters reaction. Drama is not fiction. Drama works in society on the border between fiction and reality. It uses imagination to release the mind from the emotional fixations and conceptual confusions that bind it to the past. Drama is the logic of humanness because our social reality cannot be human unless our imagination is human. So the logic of humanness is the relation between imagination and reality. And that means that the logic of drama is not fiction but reality. This is the historical lesson of civilisation. In drama the corrupting compromises and conveniences of our daily lives are confronted with our profound need for a shared human society. An animal does not need to be an animal, but we *need* to be human, and we create our humanness not when we fulfil that need but only when we make the need more demanding – when we drive it to the ultimate passions and visions of human possibility. The need and the striving explain all the twists and turns of history: the lies parading as truths and the fanaticism posturing as fidelity. And they explain the pessimism that denies the need and instead sees human beings as human wolves. Drama is the struggle to create the insights, institutions and culture of humanness.

Young people live close to the logic of imagination and drama. They have not yet entered fully into society where the need to be human is replaced by the economic need to survive and the social duty to conform. All children are creative. If they become destructive that is because their creativity has been misunderstood and frustrated. It has, ironically, been turned against them, so that (logic again) they can only turn it against others. The tragedy of history is that the destroyers are seeking to defend their own creativity.

A new drama could be created not in the market places of the media and the established theatres, but in schools and colleges and youth groups. This book is a primer for that new drama. It is in three sections. They are worked out in a way which follows the basic processes of all drama-making, whether writing, acting, directing or participating as an audience. The three sections combine the practical and the imaginative. They have the vision that I would expect from an author whose own plays lodge deep in the mind.

Our society dangerously undervalues drama's role in creating humanness. We are clever technologists and inventors but the Greeks' creativity seems remote from us – and, it is wrongly said, now beyond our reach. Yet consider a story in this book. A New York teenager kills someone in order to steal his fashionable trainers. The insights and consequences that follow from his desire for a pair of trainers to put on his feet are as profound as those that followed when Agamemnon put his feet on the sacred carpet in Aeschylus' *Oresteia*. The way the logic of drama is also the logic of humanness was shown in the 2011 riots in English cities – the riots might be called 'The Trainers Riots'. Some of the first things the rioters looted were trainers. Only drama can disentangle the contradictions in a pair of trainers and show how they contain both the loss of humanness and its recovery. The importance of this book is that the author knows it.

Edward Bond, playwright, February 2013

Acknowledgements

The author would like to acknowledge the contribution made to his work, and to the representation of that work in the current publication, by those colleagues he has worked with in a number of schools. Special acknowledgement is given to Devon Walker, Jude Ellson, Peter Wilkinson, James Stock, Mick Windsor, Stacey Morley, Jan Linnik, Alison Rudd, Darren Randle and John Hart.

At the same time, it should also be acknowledged that the schemes offered here also include ideas which have emerged from the classroom experience itself and which were first presented by countless young people who engaged in the dramas. If you were a student of Oakwood High School or Egerton Park Arts College during my time as a drama teacher, you might find your own ideas embedded here. Thank you for your energy, commitment and imagination.

A number of the schemes have their origins in the work of other practitioners who I have worked with over the years. Thanks go to Andy Jones of MMU for the roots of *Montgomery* and *Detention*, to Peter Wilkinson and Jude Ellson for *Extreme* and Devon Walker for *I, Phone/Trainers*.

Thanks also for permission to quote extensively from *Tuesday* by Edward Bond. © Edward Bond, 1993, *Tuesday*, (ISBN: 0-413-68220-X), Methuen Drama, an imprint of Bloomsbury Publishing Plc.

The book has been in development and circulation for a good many years. Over this time, many people have read and commented on it and given me very useful and encouraging feedback. I would like to thank Dorothy Heathcote, Gavin Bolton, Edward Bond, Jonothan Neelands, Allan Owens, Sarah McAdam, Stacey Morley, Ray Hartley, Hannah Bounds, Hannah Issa, Richard Taylor and Richard Smith.

Thanks also to Annamarie Kino-Wylam and Hamish Baxter at Routledge for their support.

I would like, finally, to acknowledge the contribution and impact that the work of Edward Bond, as both playwright and thinker, has had upon my understanding, my aesthetic development and upon my work as a teacher and writer. I still reel.

Introduction

This isn't a 'source book' in the sense that it aims to elaborate the sources that, say, a great work of art might have drawn upon. A source book of Shakespeare's *The Tempest*, for example, gives us reports of a Bermudan ship-wreck, or an account of the celebrity magician John Dee, inspiration for the mighty Prospero. Such source books uncover the origins of ideas. This is a source book in a different sense. It doesn't come at the end of a piece of work – a study after the fact. Instead, it aims to be a source from which new things might flow – the source in the sense that a river has a source – the bubbling spot of origin from where journeys begin.

Having said that, the ideas contained in the book are drawn from a long journey within the form of educational drama; a journey that is not yet complete but travelled enough to warrant a substantial taking of account. The book is part reflection, part personal testimony and part recounting of experiences in a modern classroom.

I have thrived on the thinking and experiences offered by the leaders of our young field (Dorothy, Gavin, Jonothan and the rest) but even as I became absorbed, there has been the nagging suspicion that their work wasn't quite *my* work. This has given rise to a subtle guilt around what I think I should have been achieving in the classroom – the purity of their work – and what was actually happening about me: something much less pure (often downright messy) but something forged in and tested against the realities of the everyday world. The beautiful and illuminating experiences of conferences, away-days and scholarly elaborations have all fed my practice, but perhaps further attention needs to be given to aligning our work. My crucible was the classroom and the 50 minute lesson. My participants were coming from geography and going on to maths, dodging wet patches and crushed chips on the dining room floor and being released in alphabetical order for their BCG jabs. I have deep respect for our venerable leaders and I hope that this won't feel hostile – it isn't meant to be – but the sense of a divergence of experience has presented me with what Dorothy Heathcote might have called a 'productive tension'; a tension that has led to the forging of the approach represented here and to the thinking that lies at the heart of the book: high concepts for our daily bread of routines.

The story of the book

The experience at the core of the book stems from the classrooms of Manchester. Here was a fascinating worksite: rich in diversity, tension, experience and complexity. Making sense of the situation – and of our work together – became the starting point for a genuine spirit of experiment: groping, stumbling forward, failing (appallingly sometimes) but hanging on to those moments of success, break-through, realisation or new understanding and slowly building a sense of purpose and meaning. It is the 'stance' of struggling for real, authentic meaning that the process of our drama aims to inculcate in our students. Experience is something to figure out, to solve. Drama is our potent chosen vehicle.

Throughout my teaching life I have kept a notebook to hand. In it have gone observations, reflections and thoughts pertaining to our work. It seemed important to capture the emerging sense. The established framework of thinking of the drama form offered an expectation of significance, and here was the working out of that significance in this particular moment and place. A salutary moment came one day when a student who must have seen me scribbling away surreptitiously found an empty page and wrote, 'Save it, ya dick!' I don't know who it was or what they had read to prompt their ire – but we should appreciate such bursting of bubbles. It anchors us to the real. Sometimes, the book still opens on the same page.

The structure of the book

The book is in three sections.

The first section looks at some theoretical thinking: a broad sweep of the educational landscape and some current concepts. It goes on to take a more individual and personal exposition of the drama experience – an approach that we've taken to calling inelegantly, 'meaning drama'. The section moves from a general discussion of the meaning of education to an account of the meaning of drama within a rigorous human-centred approach to learning.

The second section looks in more detail at some fundamentals of practice. Rooted closely in the experience of the classroom and our reflections on it are some practical, challenging and perhaps provocative ideas: food for thought.

The third section hopes to bring our thinking alive in a series of schemes of work spanning across the high school years. We hope that the schemes will be the starting point for your own further adventures in drama.

How to use the book

It is hoped that the book will be a living document; capable of growth and transformation. As the ideas and the schemes appear now on the page, they are simply just that – as they are *now*. They are part of an evolving and responsive body of work, which to remain meaningful and human must remain in a state of becoming. Both ideas and schemes are captured here as a snapshot of the land as it lies today. Like any living landscape, tomorrow it will have moved on.

The purpose of the book therefore, is to offer an insight into one practitioner's work as a way of generating new sparks of thinking and practice in the reader's own.

So how might you use it? Simple...

- Read it.
- Respond to it.
- Work with it.
- Play with it.
- Create experience to share.
- Reflect upon your own living practice.

Get in touch and carry on the discussion: john@northwestdramaservices.co.uk

Part One
Thinking drama

1 Drama and the contemporary landscape

The level of knowledge on which this first section stands is as might be reasonably expected from an alert and aware educator in the contemporary workaday setting; one in which such conceptual constructs are offered to classroom practitioners to help us to understand the nature of our work. So, a level of understanding beginning with a knowledge of the key texts, a spattering of conference workshops, a few in-service training days and some perusal of the web. Even from this lowly starting point, it seems very clear that research-based theorising about the make-up of human personality and human learning offers us the chance to look again at the purpose and meaning of drama. Perhaps even the chance to begin the journey from a peripheral activity in the institutional hinterland, to becoming a core element of a modern approach to teaching and learning: making learning matter.

For those of us with a sense of the richness of the possibilities of drama, the following collection of concepts will come as no surprise. I believe they give us simply a new set of language games to inhabit in order to speak about our work in a credible fashion with a wider range of fellow professionals. It is a new descriptive/explanatory/justificatory language that underlines the value of what we have always known through experience. From these necessarily simplified sketches we commend you to make your own explorations.

Brain-based learning

There has been an explosion in the application to learning of neuro-scientific research into the functioning of the brain. It seems perfectly reasonable that attempts to promote learning in our schools should necessarily follow the contours of the human brain as it has evolved over several million years. Our chief point of access into this area has been the work of brain-based learning populariser, Eric Jensen. And so despite this being a complex, contentious and ever developing field, there are broad (if provisional) things we can usefully say about how the brain learns, that support the approach of drama as a learning medium. With apologies to Mr Jensen and neuro-scientists everywhere, please consider the following:

- **The brain is built for activity in the 'real world' and learns best in its natural habitat.** A good learning environment offers real world challenge and real world contexts for that challenge. Good drama offers 'lived through', real world learning contexts.
- **The brain cannot escape its multi-sensory expectations** – seeing, hearing, touching, scenting, tasting, etc and combines these with functions such as remembering and processing. Good drama is a rich, multi-sensory experience that in its inception seeks to engage participants in its actions in a multi-sensory environment.
- **The brain accepts knowledge as truth only when verified by emotional experience**. An emotional experience of knowledge drives commitment to and acceptance of the learning. Good drama engages the emotions through character, situation, narrative, language; the learning experiences are *felt*.
- **The 'whole person' learns**. The greater the involvement of the whole, the greater the learning. Good drama seeks to engage with participants physically, socially, emotionally, intellectually, aesthetically, spiritually. It makes possible a total, aesthetic engagement in learning
- **The brain looks for patterns.** To the human brain the creating or finding of patterns and connections allows for the making of its own meaning. A good learning experience is an open one that offers gaps. Working to fill in these gaps, the brain forges new connections, it develops capacity – it learns. Good drama places participants in compelling, open situations which house strings of gaps – questions, possibilities, decisions, problems – human problems in a fictional context.

An additional and intriguing thought is that from a 'brain chemistry' point of view, it looks like the experience of emotion (for example, fear when facing jeopardy) in *a real* context is identical to the experience of emotion in a fictional context. Of course, our understanding of the experience will be mediated by our consciousness – we are not 'lost' in the fiction – but from the perspective of raw chemistry, to our brain, fiction is reality. This seems to add credence to the significance we drama specialists naturally give to fictional realities; in this important sense, we are not pretending, we are genuinely living.

An illustrative example from the schemes: Year 8 – *Aliens*

Miguel, our fragile, unsophisticated Brazilian peasant farmer, claims to have been abducted by aliens. We doubt him – he has too much to win by telling the story. In the teacher's simple in-role presentation of the character, the seeds of suspicion are offered subtly, by the inference of un-intentional **tells**. *He is a low status character, sympathetically drawn to elicit our care and our emotional attachment... but at the same time, our rational sense is piqued by the outrageous grandeur of his claims and the subtle doubts he sows in us. His description of his experiences is hindered by alien-induced memory loss – we leave a* **gap** *open for pupils to fill – an alien world, alien technology... visioning a possible world.*

From a 'brain-based learning' point of view we create a real-enough fiction through character, the ambiguity of the character becomes a real problem for the group – the narrative he presents is a problem for us, we must look for patterns in his behaviour to determine the truth of the story – we must read the subtleties of the presentation – our emotions are engaged as we encounter and challenge him – his story opens up a vast gap of possibility – a genuine and creative gap that the group will fill with imaginative action.

Deep learning

A powerful and very useful distinction in educational thinking has been the cleavage between 'surface' and 'deep' learning. Surface learning is characterised by tasks of simple memory, working to the test, giving teacher what she wants. In surface learning, we chew but do not swallow. Deep learning, on the other hand, takes us up the levels of Bloom's famous taxonomy: deep learning is characterised by personal commitment to the task, intrinsic motivations, the ability to respond to new learning, to make use of learning, to create our own meaning from it and add the learning to our long-term sum of available knowledge. In deep learning, we chew, taste, swallow and digest. The sustenance gained then fuels further explorations.

The richness of a good drama experience might offer a new paradigm of deep learning in the sense that the learning is approached in a significantly 'holistic' manner; I experience intellectually, physically, socially, emotionally, conceptually, concretely and in abstraction. There are many facets to the moment of learning as experienced. It is the multiplicity of aspects embedded in a rich moment of dramatic encounter that takes the learning beyond the superficial and down through the strata of significance.

Of course, there is such a thing as bad, or 'surface' drama. The kind of drama experience that relies upon closed questioning, simple, direct tasks that haven't been allowed to enter the participants in a meaningful way, that don't stop students in their tracks and challenge their sense of self or their understanding. This variety of drama is about theatrical technique or the techniques of dramatic processes, the bells and whistles of simple effectiveness. For us, it is not enough to be effective, we must be genuinely meaningful.

In a moment of meaningful drama, it is my involvement in the character, the narrative and the situation of the fiction, in a way that reaches out and grabs my full attention, which is likely to create a deeper learning experience. The situation-fed questions that might arise here are questions of reason, motivation, alternatives, possibility, consequence, significance, connection, implication. These are higher-order, creative and speculative processes that stand as emblems of deeper, richer learning.

An illustrative example from the schemes: Year 9 – *Piccadilly* (homelessness)

To preserve the 'surface/deep' distinction we will look at two experiences of approaching the same area.

A Year 9 PHSE Citizenship project

Materials have been produced by the lead teacher in PHSE – there are lists of facts to deliver and discuss, questions to ponder, exercises to do, a word-search, a video about a homeless child and a police officer with salutary tales to tell, then an opportunity for questions and (if there's time) a role play in pairs on 'staying safe' and to finish, a facts about homelessness quiz. The lesson offers a useful chance to assess some facts and discuss responses, but by comparison with the drama scheme, we might regard it as a 'surface learning experience'.

Year 9 drama scheme

Students begin with the enactment of a real event on local streets – they begin to build a sense of reality and to empathise – a character is introduced – we explore his life and our relationship with him. Questions are asked, facts embedded, characters and situations explored, felt and lived through, the challenge is imaginative, intellectual, emotional, social. We speculate, consider, confront, share, experience. The event is vibrant, alive, communal. It is a sample of deep learning that aims to place learners in intimate relation with a topic and with a narrative of significance and dramatic power.

Multiple intelligences

It is almost a commonplace now to speak of 'multiple intelligences'. When Howard Gardner first introduced the terminology into our language it seemed to have the power of revelation. 'Of course!' we cried, it seemed to free us from the padlock of the limited value given to non-academic ways of being and succeeding. It was the democratisation of intelligence. How many 'intelligences' Mr Gardner might list as a complete list, seems less important than the simple idea that *there is more than one way of being intelligent;* that other forms of excelling or simply approaching the world have validity and perhaps even equality. The approach licences the terminology of 'visual intelligence', 'musical intelligence', 'inter-personal intelligence', 'spatial intelligence', perhaps even, 'footballing intelligence'! If there are many forms of intelligence, we might argue, that there must also be many forms of knowledge and many forms of knowing. Philosophically-minded fans of rigorous conceptual analysis might baulk at the stretching of the perfectly proper notion of 'intelligence', but the new construction has such general resonance because it supports a widely-held sense of the value of a varied set of skills and propensities; the skilled craftsman, the gifted painter, the able athlete, the outstanding carpenter, the accomplished mathematician, the consummate professional tap-dancer. Where excellence is possible if seems a simple (and forgivable act) of affirmation to assign intelligence.

From a drama point of view, the language of multiple intelligence gives credence to the value of the many facets of the classroom experience. It speaks for the value of understanding another's perspective, for operating as a valuable group member, for identifying significance, for creating solutions, and much more in a list that would never be complete.

An illustrative example from the schemes: Year 8/9 – *Hamlet*

We explore the central familial situation of Shakespeare's great play; a father murdered, a mother's remarriage to his brother and killer and a son, charged super-naturally with making things right. We encounter Shakespeare's precise language and we mine the rich and complex characters for possibilities, speculating. We enter into a vibrant dialogue with the text, with Shakespeare's great mind and with each other, To be or not to be, really is the question.

From the point of view of multiple intelligence, our drama work exercises the 'linguistic intelligence' as we approach and unknot the dense and beautiful text, the 'emotional' as we consider the mental plight of the grieving youth, the 'inter-personal' as we engineer solutions to the 'narrative gap' in full collaboration, 'intra-personal' as we are invited to give private reflection to our very existence, and 'spatial' as we consider the stage semiotics of constructing the final terrible scene.

Emotional intelligence

Strongly related to the expansion of understanding of intelligence is the development of the concept of 'emotional intelligence' as developed by Daniel Goldman and others. Dismissed by some for its pop psychology flashiness, the citing of emotional intelligence does us an important service in rebalancing the tendency towards prepositional knowledge and the rational engagement with it. The allied terminology of 'emotional literacy' is equally significant in the 'felt' world of the drama classroom. We are emotional creatures; our experience of the world is mediated by our emotional being. To engage fully with the world we need to be able to understand both our own and others' emotional lives, we need to be able to recognise signs of emotional significance and to manage ourselves and others in the direction of emotional maturity.

The landscape of the drama experience is an emotional landscape. An early, essential achievement in our classrooms will be to secure an emotional response – a commitment response – from our students. The narrative development of the drama will be through a progression of emotionally defined episodes. Along the way we will explore and develop an emotional vocabulary – for our characters and ourselves; we will name states of emotional being, we will explore ways of expressing an extended range of emotions, we will experience and manage our own and our character's feelings at critical living moments, we will gain insight into another's perspective, we fill face beyond-real-but-safe jeopardy and we will prevail – living to report the experience in expressive terms.

An illustrative example from the schemes: Year 11 – *Faces*

This is an advanced drama scheme in which we enter the lives of variously 'broken' individuals; constructing their stories. Through the medium of a highly-charged self-help group we press the actor–characters into detailed hot-seating interviews. Their intimate stories are revealed. The characters are sent on a simple therapeutic mission – to engage with the world. Will they succeed?

From the point of view of emotional intelligence we explore the impulses and weaknesses of another, we press them kindly into self-expression, we find words to capture their understanding of themselves and the world, we ourselves reflect on their emotional condition and our own, we imaginatively construct another's emotional being – we master it and live it. We move towards emotional maturity, both vicariously – through the medium of character – and in ourselves.

Creativity

Ken Robinson has become a key global advocate for rethinking education along more human lines; it is a rigorous version of good old liberal children-centeredness. From the point of view of drama in education – that sounds like just where we came in. It shouldn't surprise us that Sir Ken has a special relationship with drama in education testified to in the early bullet points of his CV. In particular, as the author of the landmark 'Learning Through Drama' report. Robinson's key string of ideas might be summarised as

> *Our education system is constructed upon economic and philosophical foundations which belong to a former age. Our industry-aping schools fail many (perhaps) most of our young people. There is a terrible and destructive **lag** between our institutions and our understanding of the human animal. The rate of social and technological progress is so rapid that we cannot root our learning systems in current situations – we must create young people who are adaptive and creative enough to respond to as yet undreamt of situations. Propositional knowledge (facts) and logical forms of reasoning are not the only attributes we will need in our futures. We will need to change and respond. Creativity is crucial.*

Creativity is a key concept in Robinson's thinking. The 1998 'All Our Futures' report was a watershed in thinking about the value of the arts and creativity in schools and society in general. Along with the 'movement' of thinking represented above (and Sir Ken's never-ending, web-supported, speaking tour), it changed the cultural and political landscape in ways that still seem to be emerging.

In terms of drama, the new landscape allows us to expand the base on which we stand. Through the fictions of human life we routinely construct, we are constantly offering streams of focused pretence which require responses in a creative and dynamic fashion. The very form itself demands reactivity; as a drama practitioner, a large part of your effort in preparation and in your execution 'in the moment' is given to sustaining the dynamism of the situation; to keep it moving forward, to present new challenges, twists, rug-pulling reversals, point-blank game-changing moments of understanding.

In engaging with our living moments, students are being introduced to dynamism. They are responding to moments of change. These are behind a role, certainly, but sufficiently in the present-self to be of real use in developing change-bearing attributes and attitudes. In this sense, drama offers rehearsal for change.

An illustrative example from the schemes: Year 10 – *Tuesday*

In this scheme we explore the play's central actions: a teenage girl's study is interrupted by the arrival of her boyfriend who has deserted from the army, her controlling father will inform on him to the police. Along the way we will learn of the soldier's visions in the desert and the father's hold on his daughter will be broken forever.

We are solidly in the territory of critical moments of change; drama always operates at the edge of things where crisis elicits change. Here we are given the chance to study change, to reflect on the precipitating factors, the impact on characters and the nature of the change that is exacted after the crisis. Amidst the rich, multi-faceted drama we experience the human animal through character and in ourselves – it is front and centre to the process and to the study itself.

2 Meaning drama – a personal account

In this section we look from the previous broad sweep of generally recognised ideas, to a personalised statement of the uses and purpose – the meaning – of drama. The ideas have been formed through an amalgam of sources; from immediate classroom experiences, dialogue with colleagues, reflections on theatre and drama forms and the stimulation offered by a range of thinkers in the field of educational drama, theatre aesthetics and beyond. We hope that it will provoke and stimulate your own thinking. As a 'living' process, establishing meaning is a task that is never finally complete, but always necessarily in the process of becoming. Creating your own meaning is a task that every practitioner must accomplish for themselves and every student must be encouraged to begin. That is not to say that we are in the realm of 'private language' – that I have my sense and you have yours and never the twain will meet but – to acknowledge a truth about human living and human endeavour and human thinking – that, to repeat, we are never finally complete. We are not a 'closed' species –we are profoundly 'open'; trapped in our own freedoms. The poet John Keats coined the phrase 'negative capability' for the willingness to accept uncertainty; to be at ease with doubt, to embrace the indefinite and reject efforts to codify and capture. Negative capability is an emblem of human maturity. It is a concept that has real value in our work and speaks to the uncertainties with which we live and which our parent establishments – departments, schools, governments – need to be encouraged to recognise and value.

The following has the feel of a piece of rhetoric, but we hope it is the kind of rhetoric that we sometimes need; that will enliven our thinking and our practice. It is stridently and ambitiously expressed and you are invited to take issue with it all. Your own meanings await.

The purpose of education

At the centre of your work is the human animal and the human mind. A human mind is naturally enquiring and self-expressive, and its fundamental process is the creation of meaning. The human mind stands with capacities far beyond those required to satisfy the basic needs of survival. This over-capacity is where we find language, imagination, abstraction, self-doubt and self-delusion, expectation, hope, political structures, science and art; in short, human being and human culture. The human mind needs to exercise its over-capacity or it ceases to be fully human. It may even begin to devour itself. The human mind is hungry to learn and to make sense. A school is the site for these things; for the accessing of our accumulated knowledge by individual learners; the understanding and creativity of the species. In a good school, we encounter our invention, our sense of time and place, our imaginative production, our physicality, our linguistic capacity. In a good school, such knowledge and experience becomes part of the individual's own life and being and they are offered the opportunity to make their own contribution to the species' accumulated wisdom, understanding and expression.

A school is a human place. As teachers and students know, it is the quality of human interaction that makes for a good day; moments of meaningful human contact where something of value passes between us. A school is an important place and our task a serious one. The centre of our work is the enquiring mind and a living creature couched in a quality human interaction. In constant tension with the 'human character' of the institution is the institution itself: the structures of power, the ownership of knowledge, the control of time and the physical space, the management of groups. A wise school acknowledges the dialectic at work within its walls – and works for a maximum of humanness.

...and of drama within it

Drama, in the form represented in our schemes, takes as its starting point the expectations of an enquiring mind and the need to operate dynamically in an environment of positive human interaction. We utilise the capacity to access and maintain fictional reality as a learning tool, and we aim to create rich, human stories 'from the inside out'; offering them as 'lived through' experiences. Our dramas aim to engage and challenge in a holistic fashion – physically, intellectually, emotionally, socially, privately, spiritually. It is a highly evolved form of interaction with great potential for exercising human imagination and developing human maturity. Our range of narratives is drawn from a variety of fields – history, literature, journalism, social science, various literary genres and a touch of theatre history. We learn from inside the contexts built by the drama. Contextual learning is power learning.

Drama for meaning

The deep purpose of drama is the creation of meaning.

A human being differs from, for example, an apple (and from all other objects and creatures you might like to mention) in one important feature: a human being is human. It is the meaning-making species.

An apple doesn't create its own sense of itself. It doesn't know itself by the stories it tells of 'applekind. It doesn't call itself 'apple'. An apple is a 'thing-in-itself'. It doesn't ponder its own characteristics, it doesn't wish it could be redder, it doesn't project an image of itself out to other apples, it doesn't wish all apples to be free; in short, it isn't conscious. This, of course, is the essential and unique characteristic of being human, it almost goes without saying: we are *conscious beings.* We know that we are humanly-conscious because we speak. And because we speak, we are capable of investigating, abstracting from, developing concepts of and manipulating our selves, our companion creatures and our world. We are capable of understanding. To be more human is to be capable of greater understanding. Our classrooms should be a place where understanding reigns; where human individuals are invited to make meaning; to give meaning; to create meaning. This has always been the purpose of art and culture and of drama. In our setting now, meaning-making through drama lays claim to the vibrant heart of our educational project.

What does it mean to be a 'meaning-maker'? It means to be the centre of understanding for your own unique situation and experience; to accept responsibility for your own perspective and to value your emerging understanding as valid and significant. A meaning-maker makes connections, draws distinctions, finds expression, notices, formulates, considers, compares, captures, responds, realises, imagines, struggles. In drama, all of these happen in a social situation within imagined realities; meaning is shared, negotiated, experienced together; it emerges from the group – and the individuals take away and take forward the meanings that live for each of them. Drama is a unique and potent form of human meaning-making.

To borrow Edward Bond's terminology, human beings 'expect to be *at home* in the world' ('The Dramatic Child', *Tuesday*). We tend to peace as babies tend to quiet unless their equilibrium is disturbed by hunger, cold or discomfort. To be 'at home' we need to have our material needs satisfied, but we also need to be able to make sense of our lives. This expectation is the root of our desire to live in a just world and our need for an unfettered understanding of our situation. This means each human creature creating meaning in each human life. It is a natural process. Education can be understood as our culture's chief expression of this basic drive and need. As educators, it is also the process which we must take as our starting point.

There are many elements of contemporary culture that seem to work against us as meaning-makers. Often we are encouraged and perhaps expected not to seek understanding, but to simply consume the understanding offered to us. In this, we are objects in another's world. This is why such things as drama are such a deeply political act. In our simple, imaginative, educative and democratic acts we shift progress towards a more human, a more just culture. We move forward.

Because we are on the same journey as our students, we must make meaning for ourselves; interrogating ourselves and our situation even as we create new situations for our students.

Drama and a meaningful ambition

The pace of technological and social change within our current situation means that each new generation cannot rely upon even the immediately preceding generation's values and understandings to construct their own meaning – things move too fast. Education must seek to make people capable of surfing upright on shifting sands; creating their own meanings, for here and for now.

We have to behave in the full knowledge of our situation. This will require reading and responding to the depth and details of that situation; to our history, to our global situation, to our personal, social and institutional circumstance, to injustice, to thwarted expectation, to progress. We need a curriculum at this point that has the freedom, looseness and reactivity to approach the developing new content. Drama, with the tools that its form makes available to it, can become central to the project of a genuinely human education.

The timescale of Darwinian evolution is mammoth in its extensions back through the development of the planet's life. (Of course, in geological time, it is still the tick of a clock). But in our work it might be useful to think in terms of 'individual evolution'. In each life we should evolve: selecting attitudes which support our progress and rejecting those that tie us to the past. We aren't fixed and limited. We are in the process of becoming. Drama, as a holistic form, allows us to foster a process of challenge, examination and affirmation – a process of individual evolution. Of course, this is a process that spreads throughout the facets of a person's life and is not limited to the classroom, but here, in this empty, yawning space, where living contexts await, we can give our full attention to focusing on the processes of our evolution.

Drama and schools

We require civilised schools. A civilised school is simply one that is sincere and effective in its pursuit of the potential of its students. 'Potential' is all that a person is capable of, given the optimum circumstances. A civilised school is genuine in seeking to offer such circumstances; one that engenders faith in that potential, belief in its possibility; support for its development and love of its achievement.

A civilised school is a place of the love of human potential: individual and species. It is recklessly future-positive, even as it accepts the realities of a complex and sometimes thwarting world.

We can judge the level of civilisation and maturity of any educational institution by its attitude to and support for drama. In celebrating the human potential for understanding in each individual, and in being able to take human being as the source, vehicle and subject of its study, drama is uniquely and radically potent and inclusive. Schools need drama.

A true democracy requires dissidents. It doesn't even just tolerate them to prove its credentials, it needs them to be healthy, otherwise it becomes stolid and closed and terminal. A school is a necessarily diverse collection of people and perspectives. It needs to find space for all its constituents. A school isn't made good by management. A good school is a living organism. It needs its dissidents like a body needs its immunity. It needs diversity of ideas and perspectives and methods. Drama so often finds itself in the vanguard of institutional dissent. It always has. The structures that are brought to bear on the organisation of the school and its activities – timetables, content delineation, national curriculums, staff demarcation – can seem fixed and immovable and unresponsive to the human diversity of needs and approaches. Drama may often seem alien to these structures. A wise school welcomes the possibility of such detachedness. It welcomes the simple truth that something *different* is happening here. Were we to squeeze ourselves into these other structures, we might risk reducing or even destroying just that which makes us valuable to our young people. We must press our uniqueness, even as we develop our expertise in playing the institution's many games. This makes it essential for us to be able to speak about our work in clear, well-reasoned terms. Terms that will communicate the benefits and results of our work to those outside of our dissident circle.

But we must also serve the school. We have a unique role to play, not only as a vehicle for another kind of learning, or as a dissenting voice, but also as the gatekeeper of meaningful public performance. The theatre in our schools must create and express the spirit of the school and our work. The spirit of the school must come to be the spirit of the enquiring, struggling, hope-riddled, desperate human mind. A mind and a community free to create its own meanings. We should captain this flagship in all confidence.

Drama and the theatre form

Drama exists in the spacious world of theatre; a world of constructed fictional realities. The theatre is our home but it is a home that many of us are so often disappointed with. Does theatre reach out and speak to us? Does it challenge, provoke, enliven us? Does it reliably excite your students as your classroom might? Most theatre might elicit a tear or a grin, but is it meaningful in the sense that you aim to make your own lessons compelling and rich with meaning? Sometimes it seems that our classroom work sets a new standard for popular, dramatic meaning-making. We are theatre's lost tribe. The rest of the tribe need us back.

Much of our popular contemporary theatre has come adrift of its first impulse to create meaning. It relies on filmic spectacle, on hydraulic sets and big bangs, on bright and flashing lights and the epic grandeur of performance, on operatic emotion and celebrity magi. In other places the theatre relies upon novelty and shock or simply the soap-operas of the psychological. The theatre of our spaces is small and finite and honest and real and human. It is an experiment in meaning happening right here amongst us. There is no arbitration by production or management. There are just *us* or fictions and the meanings we will make.

The place of imagination and story in drama

For Bond, the imagination is the most important faculty we have; it is the very source of our humanity. In dramatic action, your imagination is engaged, provoked, speaks. The imagination gives us answers that spring from our deepest human and humane senses. When my imagination speaks, 'I' speak. Because of the fundamentals of our *being* – the need to be at home in the world and the place of the imagination in expressing this need – the answers that come through imaginative action will speak of justice, equality, community, peace. It is a very positive vision of our species. But the imagination needs the right kind of critical stimulus to show itself. It needs 'the gap': a space that it may open into. The processes of drama create story structures that open up such gaps for our young people. In dramatic action a conversation ensues between the teacher's imagination and the students'. The teacher poses problems for the students' imagination to answer. In turn the teacher is newly provoked. This is why it is important to reiterate that our schemes are not closed narratives – not, 'do as I say' quasi-scripts – but open landscapes for exploration.

In drama, the imagination works through story. A story is a picture of the world; one that has been constructed to reflect a perspective or open a line of thinking. In drama we need productive narratives. The stories that we tell of ourselves and the stories that are told to us in order to construct our sense of ourselves, are an important object for examination in our drama. Drama also gives us the opportunity to create our own stories – and build new understandings. In our work, we give time to the constructing of such productive narratives and we then invite our students inside, to conduct their own conversations with our narratives. Story is the key to meaningful experience. Stories in drama are open and inviting.

Drama and the technological environment

We live in a highly developed, advancing technological environment. Whether we think of inter-personal communication, access to knowledge and culture or the sharing of ideas, there has been a technological big bang, which we are still living through. One of its striking characteristics is the speed of its progress. It engenders itself with staggering pace and fecundity. Cultures are built upon technologies. Flint arrow heads were the root of a social organisation and culture, the wheel another, the steam engine another, the super-highway another. As technologies change rapidly, so does culture.

Technology contains a series of dialectics – opposites held at the same time and pulling in different directions. It might open up a vista of knowledge but separate us from the experience of it; it might open up a plethora of possible human communicants, but reduce our immediate human contact. Technology and the cultural norms that flow from it have a tendency to alienate us from our world, our immediate situation and our selves; even as they appear to unite us in new ways.

An example: In the past, apart from the incredibly rich and incredibly vain (those who might employ a portrait artist) a human life was lived with no concrete physical record of itself. Each moment came, was lived and was lost, except to memory. Consciousness-of-self was constructed by an awareness of the present and unaided memory. And so it had been for millennia. Photography arrived, and human form began to be represented to itself in stark naturalistic form, even without the intervention of the artist's eye. However, from the point of view of cultural impact, it is only in the past 60 years or so that a camera has been a household item; only in the past five that is has become a hand-held ubiquity. Now still pictures (or often moving ones) chart each stage of a human life; a broken series of images, faintly remembered. Your developing self is held and maintained. Your consciousness constructed within an awareness of a halting, discontinuous *you*. I see my landmarks captured in time. I know they are me. I gain an understanding of my progress. And perhaps I will share them with a disinterested, global audience...

The video camera is everywhere, capturing the sights, sounds and movements of our lives in rude documentary style. A child sees itself born, tastes his first solid food, speaks his first word, takes his first step, attends his first day at school. A child's progress into selfhood is no longer a private stream of impressions, but a repeatable, permanent record. Consciousness is constructed in a full awareness of the developing self: your self as an unfinished process, an historical object. 'This short film of myself, edited and film-scored, wants to tell me who I am.' In this, we have the intervention of technology into present and created self. The daily, elaborate workings out of the questions of self: 'Who I am and how I am to live?', 'To be or not to be?' seem lost. The self of the screen is a stranger to you, but it is you. Technology gives us a new relation to ourselves.

The challenge is to find a way of being human in a technological environment: to recognising the extent to which technology can intervene in our basic human relations and preserve these relations in all their tenderness and vulnerability.

So what of learning and what of drama? One of the glories and rescuing potentials of education is its humanity; the meeting of human beings in a dedicated space to speak and to listen and to come together as learners. A school without teachers is a clear possibility – particularly if we cling to the knowledge-transfer model of schooling and facilitate unfettered screen-time – certain kinds of knowledge are everywhere. But the meeting of minds and negotiation of meanings that leads to real understanding only comes with positive human interaction, with the teacher as the organiser of learning. We need to be here, now. Nowhere is this truer than in the drama classroom.

Technology can separate us from knowledge and engagement with it. I can simply consume what comes to me through the screen. I can know things by discovering their factual basis, their origins, their processes, their details, their implications. The purpose of drama can be to place us in the direct presence of knowledge and all kinds of learning situations – as thinking, feeling, imaginative, social beings. The drama classroom is a rich human space. Technology offers us encounters with knowledge and understanding; drama allows us to 'consummate' that encounter in living situations. Good drama puts us back at the centre of ourselves. It is this centring of the self (in something approximating totality) that gives drama its educative power. Drama, at its best, is 'unalienated' and 'unalienating' action. Every school department needs an ICT suite and an empty space.

Drama and democracy

The world tends towards greater justice. It is an unstoppable historic process. One that might have begun with the thinking of the Ancient Greeks or with the egalitarian notions of the eighteenth century, but perhaps it is a progressive feature of human cultures: justice as a projection – out of the structures and needs of the human animal – the need to be at home in the world.

The deepening of the reach of equality and justice has moved through our social organisations (from slavery, to serfdom, to labour to universal suffrage, to . . . whatever comes next) and through our composite cultures (race, gender, class, etc). It is a process of democratisation. Each of us can expect equality, to be valued, to be heard. Such an expectation is a bottled-genie that is now free; but it is free in an imperfect world. The expectation cannot yet find full expression, but must be worked towards. Victory cannot be assumed.

In a true democracy, we would all be agents of change and progress. Of course, our democracy isn't true. It is riddled with the shadows of the past and elements of our earlier culture cling on. But to be a democratic citizen, we all must accept our responsibilities. We must make our own meanings. Our children might receive comfort, love, even wisdom and guidance from their parents but not understanding; at least, not understanding of their very particular moment in history. Only they can create this. In being the centres of meaning-making, we should revel in the knowledge that our children are becoming more human than ourselves. They are becoming super-human before our very eyes. They are democratic citizens, moving forward together, expecting a just world.

In as much as good drama is a person-centred, socially-ambitious, meaning-making construct, it might be viewed as a new paradigm of democratic education. This is even beyond its strength as a learning medium and humanising project. Drama is a specialised form of experience that allows us to develop our unique perspectives in a supportive, corporate setting. It is a democratising process that celebrates both the individual's drive for meaning and the group's spirited dynamism. Democracy isn't about the primacy of the individual; it is about the individual's place within their community. Drama isn't about my unique perspective; it is about my own perspective as it emerges within the experience of the group. In its choice of explorations, in its approach to the individual and the group, in its freedoms to respond, in its willingness to express newly-emerged meaning, drama is a democratising tool; a tool in the developing expectation of a fairer world.

Our young people and a dramatic culture

When our drama is good, our young people are hungry to engage. In the context of the 'plastic' (in the sense of unfixed, mutable) and emerging sense of self of young people, to offer an open and humane crucible for exploration of self, situation and the world at large, can only be a service to our young people, our schools and our society.

Good classroom drama must begin where its students stand. Sometimes you will draw their attention to the world, sometimes to themselves, sometimes to the world through themselves, and sometimes vice versa. The teacher is a crucial engineer in the process of generating experience. We offer an open narrative that aims to secure commitment and engage imaginatively and will go on to place participants in the site of critical decisiveness – the site of meaning-making.

Young people and our electronic, digital culture are saturated with low-impact drama. Through it, we gain a sophisticated understanding of shallow things. Drama in schools gives us the chance to engage with dramatic media in a new way: to study it, to work with it, to master it, to create our own narratives. Good drama develops our critical capacities to take on our saturating dramatic culture.

Standing in the classroom in the midst of a good drama event, we ask ourselves: Why are our students putting so much into this work? How are they feeling? What are they getting from it? We should let them speak for themselves, but as we stand back now as observers of the event, let us hazard a guess:

> *They are feeling properly alive; charged with focused emotion. There's a meeting of aspects; feeling, thought, and body. It's intellectual, physical, emotional. It is probably unlike any other area of study in their working day. There is the element of communication; of performance, of affirmation. The students submit aspects of their own situations and lives*

into their dramas. They own and inhabit the experience in a distinctive way. At the same time they seek to be dramatically effective; to impact upon their audience. The narrative is responsive to the group and individuals. This gives a sense of authority over their work. Time flows. The session feels too short. We make the most of the time we are given.

And so...

The following is an attempt at pulling together the thinking above and drawing it into something resembling a personal manifesto; or indeed, a statement on behalf of the community I belong to.

A summary manifesto for drama

Our main claim:

> **Drama is a powerful force for enlivening learning and transforming lives and situations.**

Our claim on drama as a force for progressive development:

> **Drama promotes individual understanding and in its social dimensions, extends the reach of justice.**

Our claim on drama for educational purposes:

> **Drama reinforces learning in a full range of subjects by engaging learners in deep, brain-attuned, emotionally-rich and creative learning experiences.**

Our claim on drama within institutions:

> **Drama is a dissident area of learning that has an important role to play in a mature institution.**

Our claim on drama as a humanising tool:

> **Drama is a tool for promoting human values; its form, its subject and its values are deeply human.**

Our claim on drama and the imagination:

> **Good drama gives access to the imagination which we choose to regard as the seat of expectation and desire for justice.**

Our claim on drama and democracy:

Drama is a democratising activity which promotes the agency of the individual within the context of their responsibilities towards the group – immediate, communal, social and global.

Our claim on the role of the teacher of drama:

A teacher of drama is a creative facilitator of learning who has a full regard for students' autonomy and works alongside and in tandem with them to promote meaning.

Our claim on drama and theatre:

The theatre is our parent form and through our experiments in popular, participatory theatre we are a child who might renew its parent's world.

Our claim on the impact possible through good drama:

Good drama can support individual development, build group identity, foster learning over a field as wide as human life itself. It can promote enjoyment, joy and a spirit of seriousness about our roles.

Our claim on the nature of good drama:

Good drama strains to engage and confronts participants with incomplete, productive narratives that drive forward the drama and lead to meaning-making.

Our ambition for drama:

To become recognised for its distinctiveness, its learning, its richness and its potential. We need recognition without prescription.

Part Two
Some fundamentals of practice

The following set of thoughts is drawn from protracted reflections on the actual **doing** of drama – the practicalities and inescapable conditions of working with the form. We hope that the thinking links clearly to the preceding ideas and provides a bridge to the schemes themselves.

3 Creating compelling schemes of work

Defining the compelling

What do we mean by a 'compelling' scheme of work? Don't we simply mean a scheme that grips the attention of those taking part and motivates them to become fully engaged in the work of the narrative? The nature of this 'grip' is difficult to define, but we shall try.

The extra-ordinary

There must be a sense in which the initial presentation of the dramatic idea must be *extra-ordinary*; it must interrupt the consciousness of the ordinary flow of life and alert us to the expectation of dramatic danger. This might involve the central character and his/her situation which must be fraught with accepted jeopardy (see Aaron and Mary in *I, Phone*, or Miguel in *Miguel and the aliens*), or it might be an event that takes us to the heart of a dangerous situation (see *Tuesday*).

On the edge

The narrative should take us to the edge of things. Not shocking for the sake of the shock, but something strangely more precise in its detail. It needs the kind of shock that doesn't make us recoil and retreat, but that makes us lean forward in terrible interest. As Sophocles, Shakespeare, Ibsen and anybody else who understood meaningful theatre knew, we define ourselves and come to significant aesthetic realisations when we are brought to face the extreme. Dorothy Heathcote preferred to not speak of 'dramatic tension' – which might speak to the simply effective – but rather of a necessary 'productive tension' – a tension focused upon the opening up of thinking. Our drama must look for the appropriate degree of danger and extreme. This involves a judgement of the needs of the group and often, it also involves a judgement of the cultural limits of your situation. We push gently at the edge of what is permissible.

Lightness

Then, pulling against this sense of *the extreme* – there must also be lightness; like the dialectical of the two drama masks, this rich dynamic experience can as easily fall into laughter and frivolity, as it can into the questions of Plato. The balance is critical, as is the licence given to the group to find humour in the terrible, and the kernel of a profound idea in a simple game.

Into the gap

It is the degree to which we are able to capture students' intellectual or philosophical attention that really marks out great drama. Our narratives present questions. These are not simply formulated questions of the empathic variety ('How does it feel to be this person?'), or questions of fact or intention, they are philosophical or conceptual questions. And when we get these questions right, when the teacher and the group ease themselves forward towards a statement of this key question, it is then that we stand most fully in the gap; the question posed isn't just the question of the character, or the situation, it becomes the question of us all. It hangs before us. It is the coalescence of the dramatic, the experienced and the philosophical that gives our drama its real power and significance.

Some examples of such questioning from the schemes would include:

- From *I, Phone* – 'What is the value of a person?' or 'What is a person worth?'
- From *Extreme*, 'Does the past live in the present?' or 'What is history and does it matter?'
- From *Miguel and the aliens*, 'Is anything possible?' or 'Is human life the only life?' or 'How do you know something is true?', and
- Dare I say, from *Hamlet*, 'To be or not to be?'; with a wide existential sense given to the 'be'.

Sometimes, the narrative stops and the thinking takes over. Or sometimes the thinking is a nodal point that propels us into further drama. The idea of the narrative as an incomplete plot – or as a mystery to be solved (in narrative and concept), is very useful in sustaining attention.

Of course, it goes without saying that the point of the questions isn't to answer them, but to make them live amongst us. You might even find that the question spills out from the drama but does not even become the subject of discussion; it might be simply acknowledged and left.

The character set

A further key element in forging a compelling experience is the development of the character-set of the drama. Who will the group encounter? How will the group encounter them? How will the character's situation be uncovered? And how will the complexities of the situation reveal themselves? The group should be brought to identify with the main characters. This might be through an emotional reaction, or a sense of intrigue in their perspective or situation.

Momentum

The narrative itself must have a forward momentum; once the group is engaged, it must be taken on a journey. A key piece of learning in my own development as a teacher and writer, was the realisation that the basic building block of drama isn't the spoken word, or the scene . . . but the *situation*. We shall return to this a little later.

It should now be clear that a key set of skills in the teacher's toolkit as they come to plan for a drama event, are the skills of the playwright.

In your approach to every group there is an assessment made of just how far you need to reach out to achieve the 'grip'. Every group is different of course, but in our experience the schemes represented here have been successful in achieving full engagement over a number of years, and in a number of situations. You will need to tailor the schemes to achieve the full desired effect; this might involve toning down the entry moment or softening the character's approach, or on the other hand, tightening the grip of the moment through hardened language or cranking up the hostility towards the initiating character.

Execution – in the moment

On top of all of your conceiving and planning of the drama, the most compelling element of the lesson will be you. Everything else is important up to this point, but in the execution of the drama you must enter straight into the crucible of the narrative and demonstrate clearly your willingness to work with the group. You need to demonstrate that:

● You are fully in the moment. The drama desires your complete attention and your aim is to give it. You have locked on to the ideas, characters and narrative of the drama and your attitude displays your absorption in this joint project.

- You are willing to be a fellow traveller on this journey and willing to take on all ideas.
- The group are genuinely involved in the decision-making process that will move the drama forward.
- Although you have a well-constructed plan, you are enthusiastic about diverting from it. You have a map but there are many unknown regions on it that offer new possibilities.
- You will wonder, formulate and struggle to make sense of the unfolding drama. It is a serious matter; it is the serious business of meaning-making.
- You are also willing to laugh and enjoy the experience alongside your students.

When the drama begins, it is your responsiveness to the 'flow of mind' that ensues from the group within your dramatic situations, that will mark the success of your drama. It is this focus and attentiveness – so difficult to maintain through a working day – that exacts such a toll on the creative teacher of drama. It will be a long and tiring day; but what a day!

An approach to planning for drama

A project a few years ago, with a group of schools and university students, brought about a detailed consideration of my own planning process in developing schemes for the classroom. The codifying of this process forms the basis of this section. The process is in three parts and a summary might be of some use. The three parts are:

1. The divergent thinking process
2. The convergent thinking process
3. The dramatic structuring process.

Throughout the phases, it is important to keep an eye on your aim; to create a dynamic, human drama experience for your students that involves them in inhabiting other lives, other places and other times. This makes for rich, memorable, productive learning events.

Ordinarily, a drama teacher has no prescribed content to deliver. Drama needs the liberty of 'contentlessness'. It is the teacher's own gap which we must fill creatively. (We need recognition, not prescription.)

The creative teacher needs to operate like a magpie-eyed writer; alert for those nuggets of story from which to begin a process of creating drama. These might occur in literature, on the news, in a song, on the bus, in a snatch of poetry, in a fact gleaned from a science documentary or in a single moment that you might stumble upon in your life. A good teacher is alert to these singularities and recognises them as workable elements because they are moments that resonate for them, and might be brought before their students. Whether it be a moment of real engagement (*Piccadilly*), an illuminating image from a play (the child in *Tuesday*) or a photograph in a Sunday supplement (*Extreme*) you will want to consider how to start building out from your initial focus towards something theatrical and compelling.

So, let us look at our three part process.

1 The divergent thinking process

'Divergent' thinking involves thinking widely. Like the light bouncing off a convex mirror bulging outwards, your thinking spreads out into the world in myriad directions.

In the period of divergent thinking you are gathering together what you think you know about your chosen area of study, conducting searches for information and following where the material takes you; finding ideas, images, characters, objects, facts, stories, ideas etc that will be of use to you and your participants in the dramatic process.

Within the divergent process, a set of useful dramatic 'territories' can help to give some structure to your search. As you search consider the following:

- *Setting*: the places, or environments that might be associated with a particular theme or narrative. Your drama will need to be in a specific, real or imagined place. Sometimes a simple detail of this place can bring the setting alive.
  - A cell, Montgomery, Alabama, 1955; an alien space-ship; a peasant farmer's shack; the Piccadilly bus station.
- *Character*: the people that are evident, implied or possible in a narrative, theme, or literary/historical setting. Your drama will need to be populated by a range of people through which the exploration will be mediated. These might be the named central character or auxiliary characters with unexpected perspectives.
  - Hamlet's mother, the queen, a servant in Hamlet's castle, the grave-digger.
- *Object*: the things that are evident, implied or possible in the theme/narrative/setting. These objects may become the concrete, imaginative rallying point for your drama, building reality and commitment.

○ A handful of beans (*Aliens*); a pile of clothes (*Piccadilly*), individual character possessions (*Faces*); a few pieces of electronic circuitry (*Extreme*).

- *Image*: the images that might be embedded, suggested or conjured in the theme/narrative/setting. Images can be highly suggestive of place and character.
  ○ The sets of documentary images from segregation America (*Montgomery*), the Northern Ireland Troubles (*Extreme*), documentary images of UFOs (*Miguel and the aliens*).
- *Narrative*: the stories that are the sequences of dramatic situations that are the heart of the drama experience. They may already be there in your source or subject, they may need discovering and constructing, or the possibilities may simply need uncovering. Whichever you decide upon, they need to be made clear and present in your planning.
- *Ideas*: the big ideas which lie underneath any useful and dramatic context. What is the source/subject showing us, telling us, inviting us to consider? These might be simple, profound, open-questioned, difficult, speculative, philosophical or otherwise. They are generalised from the particular circumstances under our dramatic microscope.
  ○ What makes a person who they are? (*Faces*); What makes a person a terrorist? (*Extreme*); Is poverty inevitable? Are the poor responsible for their own poverty? (*Piccadilly*); What are the roots of violence? (*I, Phone*).

So, we have decided on an area of work we wish to explore through drama. We have begun to gather and generate ideas across the widest possible territories concerning our area of work. We may have begun to map our accumulating ideas on paper. There will come a point at which we sense that we have enough; the page may be full, our minds spent, our ideas substantial enough to be built upon.

It goes without saying these days that the internet offers an inexhaustible resource for such research. An internet search is a divergent tool. The web seems to house the sum of human knowledge and make it readily available. Our more recent crop of drama schemes have been conceived and researched online and I would now feel at a loss if the internet was not available during this creative part of the process. The screen is a window on all history and all culture. Gazing into it should be a stimulating, productive and creative experience. It feeds our imagination in preparation for the further creative task that follows. Again, technology will present us with information, the drama will make it live.

The knack to develop is the knack of honing in on the dramatically useful. These are the elements that will make your working space a thriving, intellectually and imaginatively provocative place. You will often come across facts, for example, that offer a story either by implication, their possible impact on a life or by the particularity that their generality-as-a-fact points to. Your exploratory attitude as a searcher should be 'Can I *USE* that?' Be alert for the striking, the awkward, the unbelievable, the strange, the profound, the bewildering.

2 The convergent thinking process

Once the raincloud of ideas is full to bursting (to overload our metaphors), you are ready to begin the process of convergence. Convergent thinking is thinking that seeks to end in a single result. Maths offers us an infinite selection of convergent questions: 2 + 2 is always going to be 4 (Orwell excepting). In our process here, the single result will be a linear sequence of drama activity. We have been out on our wild gathering adventures and now bring our drama 'nuts' home for sorting and arrangement.

In the convergent thinking process we are looking for connections, drawing ideas together, seeing resemblances and discarding items that don't appear to fit at this time. We might draw lines on our paper map to connect ideas or we might make a new map that is less densely populated with all that we wish to keep. We are also giving an eye to our bank of familiar drama techniques. They are always there waiting to carry us through the experience we will soon plan: vehicles waiting to be driven.

We are looking for the characters, narratives, images, ideas, objects and settings that we think we can use and work with. They emerge out of the splurge of everything. As we are seemingly programmed to do as sentient beings, we look for patterns, we wait for order to present itself, we create meaning and sense. Again, always holding in our minds the outcome we chase; rich, human experience for our students.

At a certain moment in the convergent phase of the process, our drama techniques will rise in importance as we begin to attach ideas (character, image, etc) to activity. There are many accounts of a vast range of drama techniques or conventions available. Jonothan Neelands' 'Structuring Drama' is a good starting point, though perhaps the most comprehensive list we've come across is the National Association for the Teaching of English (NATE) handbook on drama. Of course, banks of techniques are available in a range of online sites. We won't repeat these here.

Some thinking beyond the conventions might be helpful:

Fluid time

Of course, time can move backwards and forwards in a drama. A backward movement often allows us to consider the reasons for action; to ask 'Why?' with the answer being given by reference to earlier events or actions. A forward movement in time often allows us to consider the consequences of action; to ask 'If . . . then . . . ?'

Gaming

Our work in the classroom frequently uses gaming activities to introduce or energise sessions. We haven't listed these as elements, but they are important in the dramatic structure of the experiences you offer. To the teacher, a game is never just a game. It has a purpose in preparing the ground for the onset of dramatic activity; it might release energies, create commitment, draw the group together, produce focus and calm, etc. When working on the ground with a group you will need to assess the atmosphere of the group as they enter and consider using a game activity to bridge between where they are on entry and where you need them to be in order to begin your drama. In this, gaming can be a useful bridging activity. On other occasions in our schemes, a game might itself be integrated into the scheme structure to illustrate or expose an idea.

Planning and spontaneity

We plan and give ourselves the security of a known direction; the chance to think through the potential and outcomes of the experience. It is a rationally constructed context which we have tailored for our own needs and those of our group. On the other hand, we often come across the expectation that drama should be a spontaneous and free-wheeling activity. It is sometimes this expectation which holds less experienced teachers back. In our view, the ability to go 'off book', to be diverted away from a plan by a spectacularly imaginative idea from a pupil is a high-order drama skill that may come with confidence and experience and can be very exciting and rewarding, but can also be precarious. As we have said earlier, it is the potential for spontaneity that offers an element of openness and involvement to the group. If it feels right in the moment, then follow and see where you end up. But even expert practitioners shouldn't see it as a failure not to be able to follow up on ideas immediately. Great ideas should be acknowledged and pondered, and perhaps marked for storage and acted on at a later date. We give ourselves maps and might sometime allow ourselves to be led off them, or even leap off them ourselves in exuberance; but the territory of the map (your scheme) has been prepared with the care of a master craftsman. It is rich enough itself. Our planning offers wide open spaces for the group's own responses to be exercised to a radical extent. It is an open system.

But jump if you want.

3 The dramatic structuring process

Having gathered ideas, sorted them for use and considered our range of techniques, it becomes time to begin structuring the experience that you will offer to your groups.

We can think of the task of creating a drama session as a specialised form of playwrighting. All the elements are there: characters, situation, narrative development and an engineered experience for the audience. Of course, our audience in this case are also participants in the creation of the event. To use Brazilian Drama guru Augusto Boal's terminology, they are 'spect**actors**', not spectators. So, as a playwright might, we have two central concerns: the development of the narrative and the experience we are creating for our young spectactors.

Ask yourself, if you were a participant: What will I see, hear, feel, do? How will I be compelled to engage? How will I encounter the people of the story? How will the dramatic events continue to surprise and challenge me? How will I find my voice in the drama? Who will I be? How will I feel at the end? What ideas will I stumble upon along the way?

As you begin to construct the session, consider the immediate experience of your group as they move through the different activities and phases. In particular, you might consider:

Openings

The opening moments of the drama are crucial. There needs to be something which grabs your group's attention. This might be simply walking into a specially-prepared, darkened space with a pile of fairy lights glistening like a fire, or it might just be the right question: 'Have you ever seen a UFO?' What striking or engaging activity will open your session? What compelling event will introduce the central narrative, setting, idea or character? How will the participants be encouraged to freely choose to be part of the experience?

Starting where your participants are

The imaginative conversation that will be opened up through your drama event should begin from where your participants are. This could mean meeting their expectation for an energetic, fun activity, it might mean utilising their own cultural references, or asking questions that are pertinent to their situation, or which allow them to reflect on their own individual experience. Such student-centred references help to establish a sense of secure involvement. It is from this point that we can begin to take participants on wild and elaborate journeys on which they willingly bring themselves along.

Of course, we also allow for the possibility of offering students something that creates a powerful intrigue just because it is so far out of their experience.

Finding the idea

What moments will your drama throw up that make the group stop in its tracks and need to ponder the question? What questions will these be? How will they emerge? Your perpetual educator's inquisitiveness is alert to moments that invite meta-cognition – thinking above or about the experience. These general questions are drawn from the particular circumstance and open up the thinking ground to your group.

Sequencing

What is the journey that the narrative and the participants will take through your drama experience? This will be determined by the sequence of activity that you build. The following are things that you might consider when coming to sequence a drama scheme.

Simple, enquiring and imaginative logics

A drama sequence must make sense. It must be coherent. It must follow the underlying structures of things: the logic. However, its logic needn't be just simple logic. We find it useful to think in terms of three different varieties of logic.

- *Simple logic* takes us from step–to-step by asking 'What happened next?' X then Y then Z.
- *Enquiring Logic takes us into exploring* 'Why do such things happen?' 'If X, then perhaps Y, or perhaps Z . . . but why X? What happened before Y? What happens because of Z?'

- *Imaginative Logic* takes us in seemingly diverse directions informed by the lyrical or symbolic nature of the events. We are led by our intuition and our sense of right. It is the deeper, more satisfying kind of logic that takes us onto the aesthetic plane: 'I wonder........imagine if...Look...Wow!'

Finding contrasts

Throughout a dramatic construction, it is useful to consider the contrasts that are available and think about using these contrasts to maintain commitment and challenge. We provide a simple list of some available contrasts below. Consider them, use them, develop them, invent your own.

Physical ↔ Intellectual	Active ↔ Stationary
Wide in space ↔ Tight in space	Serious ↔ Light
Dark ↔ Bright	In role ↔ Out of role
Teacher-directed ↔ Pupil-directed	Individual work ↔ Group work
Doing ↔ Reflecting	Creating ↔ Performing
Energy flowing ↔ Energy held	Living through ↔ Extracting meaning

Having made all of our preparations, we are ready to begin our key creative process. Good teaching is always a creative activity. Here, we exercise our imaginative skills in a highly developed situation. Be excited by the prospect of your own creativity and the rich experience you will offer to your willing and appreciative audience.

The building blocks of drama

Situation

The situation is the basic unit of action. A dramatic narrative doesn't progress from singular event to singular event, but each event itself must be of sufficient complexity and offer a sense of jeopardy so as to provoke the expectation of some level of collapse or transformation. This must be sufficient to hold the audiences' attention. A 'situation' is a moment in which character stories, threats, ideas, nodal moments in the narrative are drawn together to form a knotty event which the audience is able to read for meaning. Each moment must be thick with tension and possibility even as it is a stepping stone in the broader sweep of the story.

Character

As Shakespeare, the master of complexity, knew, a dramatically-useful character needs to be painted so as to offer a range of possible interpretations. Good characters contain contradictions; a villain is an innocent capable of redemption, a hero is weak and capable of cowardice. In your construction of characters for the drama, think of them as contradictory entities capable of thwarting expectations. Our Miguel, the seemingly humble peasant farmer with a story to tell in *Aliens*, could be manipulating us to achieve wealth and fame, the white bus driver in the *Montgomery* story might turn on us as we cheer him on the steps of the courthouse, rejecting the role he himself has played so far. Once such complexity is built in, consider how it will be revealed through the drama. An understanding of complexity can be fostered by inviting the individual voices within the group to contribute to the development of a character in a cumulative fashion; for example, within a 'distributed hot-seat' (There is an example given of a distributed hotseat within the schemes on page 109). To accept the possibility of contradictions is to deepen our understanding of the nature of human personality. Build such complexity into your generation of character and embrace uncertainty.

Narrative

The narrative is how the stages of the story – the sequence of situations – unfold as we move forward in time. Narratives are sometimes described as 'interrupted journeys'. If Little Red Riding Hood sets out to deliver those lovely cakes and does so without incident, her grandma is happy and well-supplied with cake, but we the audience are dissatisfied. Her journey must be interrupted and interrupted with significant jeopardy. As already mentioned, Dorothy Heathcote suggests not 'dramatic' but 'productive' tension as a requirement of drama. A good narrative, like an interesting journey, involves twists and turns in the road, unexpected diversions, surprises, moments of rapid progress and speedy development and moments of standing and looking at the landscape. A good narrative keeps us on our toes.

Structure

The structure of the drama experience is the underlying architecture of the event or series of events. A good structure has a firm foundation in character and idea, to which we can return during the progress of the work. There are two kinds of structure at play in our assemblage of a scheme: the narrative itself (who the people are and what might happen to them) and the sequence of drama activities as they are offered to your group. There is interplay between the two as the structures weave themselves around each other; your choice of which might take precedence for your attention at any particular time is an important decision. The practitioner asks, Is it important to drive the central narrative forward here or to explore this moment of character revelation through the application of a drama technique? As you work in preparation and in the moment, consideration of the broad structure of the experience is central to the creative decisions you make.

Language

It is also worth considering the modes of language that are available to you in your drama. Different modes are appropriate for different purposes and to express different moments. These will be elements you consider in your planning and invite participants to become aware of as part of their dramatic study. Some of the various modes are:

- *The non-verbal language of space.* The expression of attitude, stance, relationships through arrangement in the dramatic space. Outside of a naturalistic scene we could show the relationships contained within a family, for example, in a relationship tableau. Or, of course, within a naturalistic scene we could draw our attention to the relationships expressed through the choices made about the use of space. On a stage, *everything* matters. Everything is as it is for a reason. Every element gains significance. Reading the stage is an art in itself.
- *The non-verbal language of the body.* It is said that perhaps 80 per cent of our communication is not through the words we use, but through the implications we make around those words, by our gesture, orientation and eye contact. We find that an introductory, quasi-scientific study of these elements within drama is very productive and gives us both an understanding and a language with which to speak about these things with more clarity. Reading 'non-verbals' is something we are already experts at as inter-personal practitioners – living human beings. Adding a layer of objective awareness is of great benefit. It is an easily realised emblem of our status as a specialised form of social scientists.
- *The inter-verbal language of emphasis, silence, tone.* Akin to what we routinely call 'body language' are the parts of speech that are between and within the words we speak. These are sometimes called 'paralanguage' and refer to the tone of voice, emphasis, pause, intonation, speech rate, etc.

Again, a study of these things adds authority to the understanding of our communication and can deepen the dramatic experience as spectactors.

- *Naturalistic language.* The language of everyday communication, for when it is important to register the reality of a situation. We might notice the rhythms and patterns of everyday language and note how it is different from dramatic language. We might also note that if naturalistic language is the only language we ever use in our drama, that we will be severely restricted in our expression.

- *Restricted naturalistic language.* As we become more sophisticated in our control of language it is useful to restrict language flow so as to encourage (or enforce) the conscious selection of words to accomplish a specific task. For example, you might limit a critical scene to two exchanges between the characters (A-B-A-B), or to only five words each...or one word! The process of selection is a key dramatic skill.

- *Descriptive language.* A more consciously-constructed or selected language which aims to generate a description of a place, person, event, situation, emotion. Here, language is beginning to function symbolically and metaphorically. It is becoming more vibrant, lyrical and expressive.

- *Structured lyrical language.* At certain moments of significance (which can occur anywhere within the flow of a drama) it becomes necessary and right to offer participants a formal linguistic structure with which to capture a moment or thought. In our *Hamlet* scheme this might take the full-blown form of a performance poem utilising the simple sentence scaffold of 'Elsinore, a place of...where...', but it might also be simpler in form, 'We stand for...' (in the *Montgomery* scheme). Either way, the sentence root you offer is an invitation to select and construct a more precise and higher-order expression of meaning in a theatrical language.

- *Heightened lyrical theatrical language.* The inclusion of a Shakespeare-based scheme is really an emblem of the power of theatrical language. Shakespeare is the master selector of just the right words; 'How weary, stale, flat and unprofitable seem to me all the uses of this world', 'But break my heart, for I must hold my tongue', 'Revenge this foul and most unnatural murder!' There is a depth and resonance to the selected language which lifts the dramatic experience onto a rich aesthetic level. Within our work we would wish to lead our students towards the choice of theatrical language (even beyond the proposed scaffolding) to express moments of revelation, understanding, beauty and awe. It is in these higher reaches of dramatic language that great art is possible, even in the daily experience of our classrooms.

4 Structuring the dramatic experience

Once you have in your sights the building blocks of dramatic experience, the results of your research and deliberations on your chosen area of study and your awareness of the character and needs of your group, you are ready to begin constructing your scheme. The trick (and the difficulty) is holding all of these elements in your mind at the same time as the structure of the scheme emerges. You will need to consider:

- Your initial encounter with the group – this might include an introductory discussion, a game, an alternative method of completing classroom formalities (e.g. answer the register with a statement of when you have been most scared)
- The introduction of the theme or narrative
- The 'hook' that secures their commitment
- The nodal points that deepen the response and develop involvement
- The critical points of reversal where something (or everything) changes. We alter direction and what we thought we understood about the situation is shifted and we have to think again
- The building points when the issues or problems become progressively more compelling
- The crisis points where things come to a head
- The 'get out': How do we leave this situation? Perhaps an element of summation, of final word, of personal response to the fictional journey
- Once we are outside the drama finally, how will we 'meta-cognate' on the experience? Looking back over the landscape what will we wish to say? What have we noticed? Understood? Learnt?

Managing the classroom

Drama is an activity that in ordinary terms seems to sit on the precarious edge of 'classroom control'. We invite the release of energy and promote the student voice. In other classroom situations, this might prove a test to the maintenance of order. However, we think that the form and the conditions of the drama classroom are so unique that they necessitate a rethinking of many elements of classroom practice. To encourage thinking in this area, we offer the following points of reflection:

Control and order

First, let us consider the ideas of 'control' and 'order' themselves. Order in any classroom is required for the chief activity of learning to take place. We need to focus our attention, follow a line of understanding, work collaboratively. We need a positive mental climate and the teacher needs to be positively at the helm. There is a line over which any teacher can step and beyond which control is an aim in itself; the exercise of authority becomes a target for the teacher and they revel in the sense of power. For us, this sense of control is never going to be appropriate in the drama classroom, because of the mutuality of the situation. Drama is a meeting of minds; it requires participants to bring themselves to the party and to share of themselves with the group. In the ideal situation, the control I exercise is sufficient to gather your attention together but once we move into the drama I expect to be able to surrender my authority (or at least hold in reserve) and allow the momentum of the drama to carry us forward.

Drama is a special case. There are both *necessary* and *available* conditions of the form which support the maintenance of good order and a positive climate.

Creating the necessary conditions

The necessary conditions of the form include an acceptance of a particular strain of exposure. Within a fiction in which we pretend and, on the stage on which we might perform, we are uniquely susceptible to the judging look of the 'other'. The fiction is fragile and in adopting a role we invite participants into a possibly vulnerable situation that can be shattered with the flicker of an eye. If we are to ask students to accept the vulnerabilities of the drama, we have to offer thorough, non-negotiable protection. And this must be something that is recognised and acknowledged by the group. It is a mutual guarantee of protection. This is the root of drama discipline. Our discipline is rational, humane and inescapable.

To express this line of thought positively, the drama form offers the opportunity for building a positive mental and social climate through the requirement of what we shall call (following on from the great counselling guru

Carl Rogers), 'unconditional positive mutual regard'. Whatever you bring of yourself to the drama, I will welcome, accept and enjoy. This is a powerful group-forming stance and one without which the drama experience quickly crumbles.

As a Year 10 student once remarked to me, 'Expressing yourself changes you'. Drama in schools is clearly not drama therapy but it is right to recognise that any act of self-expression has a therapeutic aspect. In a good drama event, we are in the presence of each other's deeper selves. Again, this must also be acknowledged and respected.

Drama's extreme sanction

This leads us to propose drama's extreme sanction: *It would be better to do no drama than to do drama badly*. This is just simply true. Good drama increases our sense of self, our confidence, our self-awareness, our feeling of mindfulness and well-being; it makes us *bigger*. A bad drama experience does just the opposite. It reduces our sense of self, it crushes us just a little, it makes us feel vulnerable and exposed; it makes us smaller. It is a destructive process. We would have been better to have not begun; at least we would have been as we were. It is important to have a discussion on these matters with groups and to develop understanding of the relative constructive and destructive potential of drama.

Indeed, the regular 'deconstruction' of the drama experience and the meta-cognition of responses and behaviour is a key element of managing lessons. If things do break down (as they inevitably will on occasion) to sit and speak together about the reasons for and origins of the collapse is a powerful thing. 'What is happening here?', 'Why have things gone wrong?', and 'What do we need to do to get back on track?' Of course, this is a dangerous proposition for the teacher, because it is possible that you will have to admit that it is you, or the drama itself that has led the group astray; perhaps it hasn't 'bitten' as you thought it might. Then again, there is so much that might be worth discussing about the group and the work and the day. In this mature, human situation transparency dictates that anything is up for grabs in your discussion...and who would want to pursue a drama that isn't going anywhere.

The **available** conditions of the form include the elements of the drama which themselves contain attention-sustaining potential. In particular, the almost elemental power of story, ritual and performance.

Utilising the available conditions

Story

Has a power to hold our attention that might be thought, in evolutionary terms, to take us back to our early human ancestors sitting around fires speaking of the day's hunt. Knowing those 'stories' of the availability of food and the presence of predators would have been a matter of life and death. It would have been a simple (but powerful) step to begin to recount fictional tales, perhaps with a view to explaining the origins of phenomena such as storms, drought, the disappearance of prey.

Story matters. It has a directionality that can grip us. From a successful initiation, we will want to follow the narrative and expect satisfaction in conclusion. When my daughter can't pull herself away from an episode of her favourite pre-teen comedy show in the morning – it isn't haughty disobedience or unwillingness to go to school – it is because a story has begun, and to leave the story without conclusion takes a strong pull factor. It would almost be a violent thing to force a mid-point ending to the story; such is the productive inertia of story.

So, to successfully begin a dramatic narrative has an element of control built into it. Story is a key ally in good classroom management.

Ritual

Hand in hand with story goes 'ritual'. Rituals are highly structured forms of human activity in which rules of space, movement, word, sound and character are formalised, agreed and honoured. Again, as humans, we seem to have an elemental response to ritual. We respond to the structure and the formality and once a ritual sense is established, it takes a particular kind of recalcitrance to work against the studied formality of the group.

A simple form of ritual is the entry of the birthday cake. The lights are dimmed and candles lit, the ritual object (the cake) heads the procession. The lead ritual-maker holds the cake and walks slowly forward. Our ritual song is sung and the procession moves in the direction of the 'target' (our birthday boy or girl), our ritual builds to a crescendo with the song and is capped with the blowing out of the candle and applause. This simple ceremony contains the elements of ritual, which we tend to embed in our teaching and our drama as a routine. Ritual procedures aid the development of a sense of order and expectation of meaningfulness. Indeed, ritual is the extreme form of meaning-giving to space, movement, word, sound and character, which all performance in drama is an example of.

We are talking about simple as well as complex ritual elements here. From the formation of a precise circle, the formal taking of registers, the entry into a darkened room in silence, the playing of a game with dramatic tension, your delivery of the story set-up in hushed tones, through the ritual-supported performance of scenes, to the enactment of the rituals of a courtroom, or a burial. It is worth taking the time to establish ritual practice properly.

Our 'ritual' in the classroom is an emblem of meaningfulness. A class that masters the performance of ritual and honours its use is a class ready for real drama.

Performance

Performance has something of a chequered history in educational drama. It seems to have felt necessary at some point in the development of the form to distinguish 'drama' from 'theatre' and 'performance' was a useful point of distinction. Drama wasn't about theatrical performance, which was thought of as a kind of showing off, and quite rightly, since there is a variety of narcissism involved in some kinds of performance. Drama was something else; drama was a form for exploring human life in a dynamic fashion but not for creating public performance. This tended to create a peculiar separation between educational drama and its natural historic field. However, more recently the division between drama and theatre has tended to be bridged by a recognition of drama's place within the field of a wider dramatic culture and through the practical demand for performance in the flow of classroom activity.

You will see throughout our schemes that there are regular opportunities for some level of performance; not public performances, but internal, formal sharings of the product. We shouldn't be afraid of this but make use of the structural dynamism that the prospect of performance gives to our work. When we are preparing for performance, we are driven by the imminent special attention that our product will be given. In a positive social climate, such performance will be nodal and a staging post in the development of meaning. It shouldn't be forgotten either that as students work between themselves, for example, to answer a particular point of contention within a drama, they are not only developing collaborative skills but also taking full ownership of the thinking of the drama and the narrative itself. A well-received performance is a moment of affirmation and a test of the level of absorption in the narrative. Performance and the whiff of romance that surrounds it is a powerful element for sustaining interest and commitment, and a useful tool in positive classroom management.

But we can go much further in thinking about the significance of performance. Human beings have obvious physical needs but they also have social needs; including the need for recognition; the need to be affirmed by others. Recognition and affirmation are why performance matters. The struggle for recognition is often the root of tension and conflict between individuals and groups of people. It is also the root of the impulse to express oneself and love. As social beings, we crave the look of the other. The desire for wealth and fame is a distorted need for recognition. It is an inflated super-recognition. When we think of students performing we should not think of vain, narcissistic super-recognition. Recognition is a simple, honest need and should be respected. It is a significant factor in the positive spirit that often surrounds drama as a subject. In the drama classroom, I do not seek recognition by reference to my looks or my social standing or my wealth or my possessions or my strength; I seek recognition by the bald fact of my humanity and by the fact of my standing upon the stage before you. In the drama space, your support for my acts of recognition is a given.

Performance matters because the self, the imagination, needs a space to speak and to be known. In a theatrical form, there is no avoiding performance. What we need are well-managed, meaningful and positive performance opportunities. Students should be encouraged to perform and perform well. The distinction should be between good performance and bad performance. Bad performance is narcissistic and involves artifice or inauthentic behaviour – showing off. The performance in a drama classroom seeks authenticity and not artifice. It seeks to share the emerging understanding or new aspects to the narrative. In performance mode, the actor is an agent taking responsibility for meaning and expression. Not objects in someone else's created world, but subjects in their own.

We live in a dramatised world. We 'perform' to fulfill complex social roles in our ordinary lives. Such an idea of 'performance' is a part of drama's field of interest and through studying, reflecting and practicing a range of modes of performance, our students get to develop expertise in all forms of human interaction.

Understanding behaviour

In approaching the management of the classroom, it can be useful to accept that as with crime, all misbehaviour has meaning. All crime and all misbehaviour is symbolic. In the classroom, all our behaviour becomes a subject for exploration. The effective drama classroom is a place of a special kind of surrender.

In many circumstances, the disruptive behaviour of students results from their transposing behaviours which are conditioned by other circumstances within the student's life (a challenging home or on the urban street) into the classroom setting. The drama classroom must be a place where they can surrender their other roles in order to inhabit new ones. There is a special kind of freedom and progress in this.

The recognition of alternative ways of being available within the drama classroom must stand as an alternative to destructive forms of social and personal recognition. Many of our participants in high schools will be living through the emergence of self before our eyes. Students will also often experiment with extreme versions of adult roles. It is a struggle with identity. Within drama, students are offered the freedom within the fiction to abandon their experimental roles. They come to know that their social roles are experiments in identity and that other experiments are also possible. They come to know that the role they may think they have to play is fully within their own control. The swaggering, disinterested anti-learner is not all there is. Drama can be the place to explore other possibilities. In drama, I am only a possibility.

The drama teacher

A good drama teacher should offer an immediate and present example of the striving, aware, mature human individual. Drama teachers should be sure to present themselves as creative individuals. They should feel the freedom to create their own meanings and interrogate their own situations. Their aim should be to create a thriving daily culture of meaning-making through drama.

An expert in the field

In martial arts instruction, the 4th-dan black belt teacher carries her authority and her knowledge in her body and in her look. We recognise and honour her expertise. We respect her potential to liberate us from the limits that bound us. We know that she is well practised in her art and that she is there to share her expertise with us. I would like to say, 'I am a black belt in drama'.

The teacher is an artist. Not, for example, an actor who teaches, or a writer who teaches but, in the execution of their teaching, they behave as an artist. A teacher takes creative action to manipulate the chosen resources to create meaning through artistic form. To the drama teacher, this entails the use of narrative, character, situation, voice and movement in space to create imaginative and meaningful experiences for participants. A good drama teacher is an artist who is a full 'agent' in the world; a subject struggling to make meaning; an artist who has to leave themselves peculiarly vulnerable to the world; to choose to inhabit a vulnerability that is perhaps (dare we say) akin to the innocence of childhood. This is a possible source of the empathy that can develop between the artist-teacher and the child-participant. The drama teacher is open to playfulness, sometimes irreverence, fun, and is keen to show their pleasure in their play. Good drama is work-full play; or playful work. Although the drama teacher is clearly the adult authority in the situation, and the representative of the institution, there is also something of a productive tension (a dialectic) between their role within the institution and within the drama. There is often a detachedness. This is a good thing. Both drama teacher and child are subject to the authority but also observers of it.

The general detachedness of the artist is not a peculiar mental aberration; it is not an encoded trait of personality. It is simply an acceptance of our existential situation as human animals and the basic condition of the pre-socialised child. This existential separation is an attitude of mind that can be developed or taught as a stage in developing maturity. Or rather, it is an attitude of mind that can be re-awakened or supported into long-term sustenance.

Drama teachers:

● Are creative artists who set out on a journey of investigation with fellow learners
● Have their skills – theatre and drama amongst them – but their skills aren't the content of the work of drama, they are the tools for creating meaning through drama
● Exercise their own understandings every day in the community of the classroom
● Must be willing to sacrifice their knowledge and experience in the service of the student. The sacrifice of self is sometimes the price we pay for the student's creation of their own meaning.

A good teacher develops an instinct for creating the meaningful experience of the classroom. The best drama teaching is a personal, creative act. Within the flow of ideas there must be space for change. New ideas and characters and situations emerge, the events of the world give a new meaning or interest. Teachers create on their feet; in the moment. Ideas flow. In the exchange teachers surrender their ideas when others occur and allow the new thought to run.

The teacher's 'psychic size' and strength within the classroom is inversely proportionate to the space created for students. I can be too big. A teacher's ideas are never more important than the students'.

The teacher knows she can herself create; she has exercised her imagination and has hourly opportunities to express it. The students have just this hour. They are feeling their way and need this time and space.

A teacher may speak in unacceptable terms; in provocation; in strident slogans where the mission is clear and the developing, discovering and holding of ideas is modelled. A good teacher effectively models bewilderment, disbelief, surprise, illumination, the struggle. Teachers are driven by a love of human interaction; the interaction that creates meaning being the most powerful, rewarding and addictive. A drama teacher is a struggling mind in a place of struggle.

If you want to I know who I am, ask my students.

And so to ground with a bump . . .

5   Assessment in drama

The peculiar nature of the subject of drama gives rise to a range of issues when it comes to formal assessment processes; particularly, when the formal model of assessment has not been rooted at its inception in the realities of the drama experience. Of course, assessment, reporting, examination are all part of the game we operate within, but, as in all things, it is an important part of our situation which should be open to reflection, and for which we reserve the right to take a considered stance. Of special interest are the issues of observability, judgement and the significance of the group. From a discussion of these things we will move to the consideration of a workable approach to assessment that perhaps we can live with.

Observability

A meaningful dramatic experience impacts upon those taking part. In the best situations, the impact is upon actors and spectators – and, for us, spectactors – alike. The impact, however, may not be observable in the classroom. The impact may not even be 'state-able' in the social situation of the classroom. To do drama well, we have to accept its grounding in complex experience and we have to accept that the impact may be equally complex and unobservable. In the moments of our best dramatic experience a plenary would be crass. The best plenary is sometimes silence; and the best circumstance for it to happen is with the disassembly of the group.

In common with other art forms, drama chases aesthetic experience; the moments of silence and awe and wonder and understanding that drive creativity. We believe such 'high-order art' is possible within the classroom and the 50 minute lesson. In careful hands (our own and our students) we can stop time. There is technique and skill to be learnt, but this is not the substance of the experience. Furthermore, as detailed earlier, drama uses the individual self in a unique way and may affect attitudes, understandings and feelings that are central to the student. The 'learnings' in this situation may not be observable in the classroom even though they may be carried into the student's life. In short, the substantive work of drama is often private. In assessing, we can only objectively judge the observables. What matters in the experience may not be observable or assessable.

Art is a way of knowing. The knowledge and experience that comes through the language of art cannot always easily (or usefully) be described in the languages of other forms of human activity; number, quantification or pre-assigned statement, for example. Art must be allowed to speak for itself. In reality, the closest we can get to the true assessment of art can only be an elaboration of the experience of it, and we would probably need the expression of other arts to capture that experience; a poet to assess a concerto in poetry; a dancer to assess a sculpture in dance. If it is art, it reverberates within our selves. We let it out in new expressions; in new art. Our art is drama. Drama operates through experience. The external manifestations of experience (from which we might infer a host of impacts) can be observed but not meaningfully quantified. If our assessment processes rely upon quantification, they will simply miss the mark.

It is important to see this not as a limitation of the subject but as a simple feature of the complex construction of human experience that our medium is.

Judgement

Schools, as functioning institutions, supported by ICT-led systems, can only function in important areas by reference to the absolutes of the quantifiable – of measurement. 'Measurement' is a quantitative concept; it is concerned with the length, breadth, height, weight etc of a thing. 'Judgement' is qualitative; it is concerned with the value, quality, significance of a thing. It seems to be the need for inputted data that distorts assessment and leaves experience-based subjects with a misalignment of the experience and the recording of the experience. This is not just true of Drama but PE, dance, elements of hands-on technology, creative aspects of English, etc. By insisting that the assessment of your students and your work as a teacher be carried out as a 'measurement' necessitates a limited category of possible assessment approaches. In philosophical terms, it might be considered a 'category mistake'. This is where confusion occurs because a concept relevant to one category of thing is mistakenly applied to a thing of another category. In this instance, the concept of measurement is misapplied to a judgement of value – as if we could measure value like we can measure length – which, of course, we can't.

In most institutional assessment processes we are in the sphere of the observable, the countable, the definable. We measure when we should judge.

We know why this is the case, because institutions tend to assign administrative solutions to human problems. Administrative solutions so often
necessitate data relevant to statistical analysis. For us, the human problem is
capturing progress and learning in a living situation in a meaningful way. All
very well, but what approach should we take with the operation of our work
within educational institutions and their processes?

The significance of the group in drama assessment

In normal circumstances, assessment tends to reference the individual in
isolation from the group that they operate within. This might be called
'atomisation'. Although it might be considered important to track the
development of individual students for many reasons, we believe drama should
speak up for the significance of the group and group learning. Perhaps a good
analogy is with team sports; the crucial thing is how the team performs, and
although we look carefully at individual contributions to the team effort, the
quantifiable element is the success of the team. In sport, it is possible and
expected to say, for example, 'The team played well', or 'The team has learnt
a lot'. The group is spoken of as having an individual identity; and this doesn't
feel odd. We believe firmly that the group should be afforded corresponding
legitimacy as an entity capable of learning, behaving, considering. We must
accept and take as legitimate 'group achievement'. The work of the 'group' will
be the cradle of success for individuals, but is also capable of success itself. I
can achieve as a group member though my contribution may be indivisible from
the group itself. The 'movement' of a group, of a community, is an important
social and dramatic action. The sense of humane, corporate work and mutual
support is a goal and a necessity for good drama. Group learning is a legitimate
aim. As is group spirit, group transformation and the transformation of the
individual by the group. Within assessment in drama, reporting on group
achievement should be an acceptable routine.

A workable approach

So how will we proceed? We offer the following approach.

Speak to policy makers

Affirm in your own thinking the issues around assessment in drama and seek
opportunities to have respectful, professional discussions with the policy-
makers and leaders of assessment in your school to, at least, raise the issues.

Be clear that you are not trying to side-step or avoid assessment processes, or to cause trouble, or to make special pleading, but simply to explain the issues from your standpoint as a drama specialist. Invite them into your classroom to afford them an understanding of your realities.

Look to local requirements

Look carefully at the requirements of your school's assessment processes. What is required and how can this be achieved without impacting upon the delivery of quality drama provision? Can the processes be used to support the sense of affirmation embedded in drama processes? Your students will be well-versed in the game-playing aspects of assessment; be honest about your hesitations and have rounded discussions with them about the processes of assessment in drama.

Establish the reflective stance

Make the reflective stance a commonplace feature of your classroom work; we are engaged and absorbed, but we also step back from such absorption and reflect as a group. Not only on the dramatic moment but also on our responses to it and the impact it might be having on us. What are we thinking, feeling, understanding about this unfolding event? This is distinct from the explicit, 'today we will learn this' approach. When we create the experience we have a sense of the territories it might take us into, but we are also prepared to be surprised.

Capturing thinking

Establish the group reflective session as a part of the structure of sessions and consider ways of capturing and recording this thinking.

Create a record of your work

Consider the use of ICT and digital technology to support the mapping of drama experience and the evidencing of experience. You might think about making discreet recordings of your drama sessions. In our experience, video recording (because of the directionality of the camera lens) impacts upon the experience in an unhelpful way. It adds self-consciousness and anxiety. Audio recording, however, can be done discreetly but will still provide a record of the experience and the involvement of the group and individuals. Digital audio files are much smaller and more manageable than video files and you might make a library of lessons over time. These can be used as evidence for external agencies and help you to reflect upon your own work. You might permanently establish a simple microphone and recording facility in your classroom and establish protocols with your classes about when recordings are taking place. You might consider just recording reflective sessions or select periodic sample recordings of whole lessons.

Consider how you might gather on-going individual responses to your work together. Perhaps through individual drama journals that students are encouraged to personalise and complete regularly at the end of or between sessions. In a very successful experiment with Year 9 classes, I entered into meaningful written dialogues with groups in which students wrote regularly at their own discretion (there was a minimum requirement) and every few weeks I took in a selection of journals, reading and responding at length to their thinking. It is important to consider here that your drama together must be of sufficient strength and impact to generate a high level of thinking and response; it must be sufficiently provocative. You might also 'frame' the questioning and reflective focus in your sessions in order to scaffold responses. The journals must be established not as accounts of what happened, but as reflections on the significance and meaning of what happened. What questions arose and how do you respond to them? What is your attitude to the characters, their actions, their relationships? Does the drama make you consider aspects of yourself or your life or your thinking? What of this would you like to share?

Create summative assessments

You might also make use of online facilities for gathering thinking; a programme of online blogs that students might access in the class or remotely. The blog itself might offer some simple responsive structure but should be phrased so as to encourage reflection and not description.

An interesting development of this might be to make a video or audio blog an option. Both of these options offer a different mode of access to students, which might reflect the differing preferences of learners. The invitation to record and upload speech would offer access to a different level of consciousness and perhaps a new depth of response. Again, your drama had better be powerful enough to warrant such procedures and generate such responses. Writing in response to the drama will only be a meaningful activity (and not a homework chore) if the drama that generates it is meaningful itself.

Generate outcomes

Within your drama planning, consider opportunities for generating outcomes which can be stored as evidence of the work and might be assessable through the criteria of other subjects. Two examples: an inmate's letter to her mother written within *Detention* (a piece of writing in role) could be kept as evidence and paired with a part of the student journal, or it could be videoed to form part of an on-going blog. Also, monologues that were written within the *Faces* scheme have been used as high-grade submissions to GCSE English examinations. Perhaps you could consider finding a way of formalising this possibility by working in partnership with your English Department. It might need to be at arm's length, but it could be to your mutual benefit.

Create end of scheme assessment

Introduce the process of 'End of Scheme Assessment' tasks. We have included some of these in the schemes. In this way, students are given the chance to work in a more self-directed fashion to meet a specification that will show their learning. Each assessment task is designed in order to summarise the possible learning and lines of thinking of the scheme. In addition, challenge groups to produce a piece for performance and assessment. Normally, when using these summative tasks with classes I would tailor them to capture the development of the scheme for each group. This means that whichever direction the work might have developed is represented in the scheme assessment; it will, therefore, be tailored and edited at the last possible minute. What we offer are starting points. These assessment tasks are very welcomed by students, who enjoy the space for their own creativity and working towards a performance. It satisfies your students' desire for protracted small-group play making and, given that you might play the full game and give marks or grades for these semi-formal assessment occasions, it satisfies the school's (probable) love of data!

Tailor your handbook

Within your department handbook, you might consider inserting your own formal commentary on assessment (as we did in ours). Perhaps it might run as follows:

> *Whilst we are willing enough to make use of the required assessment*
> *frameworks already in place within our school we would like to note that:*

Drama makes demands upon the individual 'self' quite unlike the general work of many other subjects. Students are required to use themselves, their lives, their thoughts and their feelings as raw materials for the work. This powerful sense of recognition and affirmation is one of the attractions of good drama. However, it does sensitise the whole issue of assessment. What we try to create is a community of mutual support, in which students are protected during their moments of sharing and self-expression. What we wish to promote, are far as it is possible, is a situation of 'unconditional positive mutual regard' (after Carl Rogers). This is the most valuable device we have. It means, therefore that any assessment taking place must seek to maintain this. Our assessments will mirror the form of school-wide procedures but will take as their guiding principles that:

> *Assessment is a stage in the process of self-affirmation and will, wherever possible, be expressed positively, giving special regard to the student's willingness to participate and to support others' participation.*
> *Assessment in drama makes no claims of objective appraisal. The point of reference must be each student's prior attainment and not the mean attainment of 'the group', local, national or otherwise. Our central concern is the students' developing view of themselves and their world.*

> *Alongside formal assessments, we will aim to gather a multiplicity of evidence which will spill naturally from the drama and aim to represent the work of our classroom in all its richness.*

In all external assessment for examination purposes, we will rigorously apply all the criteria given.

6   Some thoughts on our art

The classroom is an everyday place. We work in time compartments in system-generated groupings. Much of our work will be routine and pedestrian. Let us be honest. But in these pages we speak of something else; of deeply serious moments of revelation and illumination. These are grand concepts (and easy to write) but is life-stopping aesthetic experience possible within our daily routines? The purpose of this book has been to raise the conceptual stakes in our thinking around drama and to draw attention to the possibilities of daily classroom experience. At the very least, every day we should be capable of engaging enquiring minds and offering stand-out experiences that lift students' sensibilities, enjoyment and intellectual perspicacity. That leaves them at least slightly more *alive*. But we should also be ready to recognise moments of our own strand of aesthetic experience; a strand appropriate to our peculiar form of youthful, participatory art. We should look out for the following, which can be seen as emblems of our aesthetic experience:

Flow

When we loose track of time and the lesson is gone before we know, it we have entered into a period of 'flow', which, as described by Mihaly Csikszentmihalyi, is a mark of the achievement of an optimal state of absorption and happiness. In drama terms, we may have become immersed in a character, or in a moment of whole group drama; the narrative, our response to it and our thinking around it has gripped the attention of the group. We may operate as a single unit and the momentum of the drama takes us forward. Such absorption and loss of the sense of self is a mark of the aesthetic.

Illumination

Illumination occurs when an event or moment stops us in our tracks and we suddenly realise something to be true. Sometimes this can happen for the group and you remain a spectator, but sometimes a realisation takes you by surprise as well. These moments might engender head nodding and 'Ahhh' and an excitement to speak about the realisation, or they might be followed by silence . . . because we all understand without the need for response.

Silence

A special kind of 'full silence' can follow moments of dramatic artfulness; we hold our breath and our eyes widen. This is the gentle breath of awe. We don't want to move. Something about the dramatic moment – a word, a phrase, a gesture, a movement, a look – is read as a full, perhaps symbolic capturing of understanding. It is a moment of communion between the deeper senses of ourselves – root imagination to root imagination. It is beautiful. I could describe such classroom moments to you: a Year 9 class rendering Rosa's prayer or a Year 4 boy speaking an improvised monologue as Queen Gertrude using Shakespeare's language pattern or Year 11 Craig sitting on a dusty floor and speaking Irene's speech to the police woman in *Tuesday*, but it wouldn't make any sense to you. You might not even believe me. But such silence is real. It occurs when a hundred disparate elements suddenly gather together, when patterns merge and draw our full attention to just this moment. After the recent performance of a precise and beautiful devised scene on *Hamlet*, (as illustrated on our book cover) we noticed that time had stopped.

Meaning

And of course, the final mark of the significance and aesthetic of our work, the making of meaning. Just the right words are found, a formulation of words spills out of the moment and crystallises meaning. Sometimes, the understanding generated might not need articulating; it may be understood on a super-linguistic level. And sometimes, we might know that an event of significance has occurred amongst us and walk away.

Other ideas from the drama classroom

Being in a drama classroom shouldn't be like watching television. It should be like going to the fair.

The drama classroom has its own rules; renegotiations occur. School rules are honoured as necessary but suspended if required. The new rules grow from the dramatic activity.

There is a moral imperative in the drama experience. Because I speak I expect to be heard. I expect to be listened to. By extension, when you speak I will listen. Mutual regard is inherent. When I seek your attention, I expect to be seen and to be listened to. This is the root of our positive moral climate.

Drama can sometimes seem like another branch of the entertainment industry, and there's nothing like it if you crave popularity. But, then we are lost in the circus of noise and energy and fun. There is nothing wrong with these things in our classrooms, but they are the preamble to the substance. Lightness is the dancing-free before we can stand still and look at the world clear in the face.

On the effective and the meaningful

It is easy to be effective; to push the right buttons and create emotional or theatrical impact. It is a technical matter. Sometimes, being effective might be a staging post on the way to meaningfulness, but meaning is the aim; for the creator and the watcher.

Drama can be effective but not meaningful. It can be 'tabloid' drama. It is meaningful if it is able to speak to the participants (and audience) about their situation: if it communicates a particular perspective that adds to their general understanding.

We must be open and vulnerable and accepting of uncertainty; that is our strength. The attitude of mind we seek, that is most human, is one that interrogates respectfully, that questions urgently, that listens carefully, that accepts courteously, that creates honestly: one that is a 'subject' in its own life. One that is free to understand.

The end point of your work is to give students the skills to make their own effective and meaningful drama: to speak; to bear witness to their lives.

You are invited to join in with the on-going evolution of our work. Get in touch: john@northwestdramaservices.co.uk

Part Three
The schemes

Introduction

The schemes are offered as the 'working out' of the preceding ideas. They are experiments in meaning-making and vibrant classroom learning experiences within the setting of the secondary school.

Each of the schemes has evolved over fifteen years of practice. They are the result of exploration, mistake and accident; student imaginings and staff suggestion; a decade and a half of dramatic conversation within a contemporary urban setting. The experiments continue. The schemes are an invitation to join both the experiments and the conversations. In the delivery, there is always compromise and diversion, school bells and dinner-ladies, exhaustion and failing faith. It is only ever this clear on paper.

We have chosen to express the schemes as a continuous series of numbered paragraphs. We think this allows the schemes to be tailored to differing circumstances. You will find your own stopping points and natural breaks. The schemes have run as full day workshops, in three-hour blocks, or more normally, as a six- to eight-week scheme of work, within hour long slots.

Our assumption will be that most readers will be familiar with the basic approaches and techniques of the field and will be able to grasp the flow of the scheme as it might operate in their own classroom. You might be an experienced teacher, or new to the profession, or, indeed, an English specialist looking for insight into the active approaches to drama, but we shall assume that the fundamental elements are secure in your mind. These accounts of experience are a living thing; what we offer are not scripts for teachers to follow but possible structures of experience that you are invited to make your own.

What they don't include are all the necessary preparations and dressings. For example, warm-up activities, games, anecdotal diversions, unintended comic asides, the moments of lightness, humour, digression, energy which will form an important element of the positive, human experience that must thrive around you and the work.

Many of the schemes originate in or contain ideas from fellow drama practitioners. In particular, I would like to acknowledge Devon Walker for early thinking on *I, Phone/Trainers*, Andy Jones for the seeds of *Detention* and *Montgomery* and Peter Wilkinson and Jude Ellson for providing elements of *Extreme*.

Enjoy the ride.

Year 7 scheme: *I, Phone (Trainers)*

In this challenging scheme of work students are invited to consider a number of areas: the significance and importance of consumption and technology in their lives, its impact on human relations and the roles of consumption and 'possession' in their sense of self. In the later stages, questions of criminal responsibility are drawn out. On one level it is an exploration of the 'cult of the brand' in our society and the pressures of needing to 'own' in order to be of value. On another, it is an exploration of friendship and family life in the contemporary setting. It should not be a simple paternalistic critique of the situation, but much more importantly, an exploration of what it means and how it feels to be a young person (and a parent) living under these conditions. The scheme creates two characters as a tool in this very private exploration and loads student's reactions onto them.

In his introduction Edward Bond refers to this first scheme when he speaks about the New York teenager and his trainers. The scheme has a long history and for most of its life the narrative was built out from this real incident. In more recent years, we have updated the key object to become a mobile phone. Even more recently, I visited a former school where the original 'trainer' scheme is still exercising its power as it ever has. The choice is yours.

Since the original work on 'Trainers', things have moved on apace and as I speak, (but perhaps not even as you read), it is the mobile phone that dominates. These immense and even beautiful pieces of hand-held gadgetry are packed with more than a pre-digital dinosaur-mind like my own can grasp. They are key objects of desire, key centres of entry-level consumerism and key tools in our new relationships with each other and the world at large. In this scheme of work, the element of possession and personal value remains intact – though the object is a new one. In years to come, and in your own situations today, you will need to amend, extend and keep up with the rapidly changing gamut of advances and value-giving of your own young people. The human story of value contained here will, we expect, be pertinent for a long-time to come.

The bare facts of the Aaron story in which an American teenager murdered his best friend to steal his trainers were told to me in about 1990 by Devon Walker, my first, inspirational Head of Department in Manchester. Devon was using the story in his drama classroom. At the time it was current news. The story as it stands below has been recreated in the telling and in the responses of students over the intervening years.

When we first started working with the story of the young New Yorker, we had no obvious way of tracking down the original details. It came to me as a story overheard. In the circumstances, such vagueness seemed to licence our own elaboration of the story. The main character became 'Aaron' for reasons of cultural neutrality. Now, of course, we can find out the details of the originating story in the blink of an eye online: names, circumstances, facts, interviews, photographs. We can be precise and factual. Of course, you are welcome to do this research and build out from the results... but we haven't. We have left the narrative development just as it was in the long, classroom evolution of the scheme. We have respected the contribution of different groups and the successive moments of development that have survived into this telling of the scheme.

Phase 1: Setting the scene

Part One: Exploratory discussions

1. Begin by asking the class for help. To launch a new drama you need information which you don't know but which students do. Introduce the question within a story.

2. Imagine: I'm 13. My mum went out on Saturday and bought me a mobile phone. Can you believe... I've never had one before. She bought the best she could find. Money was no object. Now tell me: What did she buy and how much did it cost? Will it have been on a contract or phone only on pay as you go? Allow students to discuss between themselves and then with you. Encourage excitement and moderate competition for ideas of relative value. Work towards a consensus. Note the names and amounts mentioned.

3. Now begin to approach the character you will soon play. Explain ashamedly: The truth is that your mum went out on Saturday with the money she'd been saving to buy you a phone. You'd been pestering for months. **What had you been saying?** Invite replies and expressions of the

pressure you put on your mum. Listen to as many as seems appropriate. She brought the phone home and put it on the table: still in the bag. Produce the bag and act this out in the centre of the circle. Quickly ask for a volunteer to come and play 'you' and 'your mum' in the simple enactment of the scene. You have your back to your mum so she can't see your reaction. Did you do that on purpose? Why? Build tension anticipating the reveal of the phone. When you looked (look inside the bag) you could have cried. **What did you think when you looked inside the bag?** Thought-track a number of suggestions. **Why did you turn your back to your mum?** Discuss possibilities: anger, not wanting to hurt her feelings, shame? Now narrate as the actors act: 'I opened the bag and looked inside... I took out the phone box.' The phone is a cheap, low-functioning 'brick'. Discuss: Does it matter? How did I feel? How will I feel? Will I reject it? When I turn around to face my mother, what will I say? Invite suggestions on this. Return to questioning the class: What phone is it? How much did it cost? Again, allow students to discuss with each other and with you. Expect possible hilarity as you discuss these low-status items, but return the focus to your character's sense of disappointment and dread.

4. Having determined the class' idea of the least credible phone, move towards the first large-scale dramatic situation: a teacher-in-role drama (TIR) in which you will play the pupil just introduced. You've been talking about getting a phone for weeks. Your mates have been winding you up and advising you on the best you can get... like theirs perhaps. Everybody's got one! Your mum has brought you this phone – you couldn't reject it, and it is now the moment you have to take it to school for the first time. Question the class again, this time within a prescribed structure. If you were this character how would you feel as you leave the house? If you were the character's mother how might you be feeling as you watch him go? The class answer in each case by completing the sentence root 'I'm leaving for school and I feel...' and 'I'm watching him go and I feel...' You might invite each speaker of a line to enter the circle and create a 'stance' or 'tableau' for the character to support the line they say. Consider how diverse their suggestions might be.

In this first part you have engaged with the students' world, asking them for knowledge and insight. You have given students' knowledge status. You have also anticipated the teacher-in-role scene which follows. You have also begun to develop an emotional vocabulary and to build a complex productive tension into the characters and their situation.

Part Two: On the school yard (teacher-in-role)

5. Build the situation. It is Monday morning. We are in a school playground. The class are put into four or five smaller groups and each group creates a general tableau of students in a school playground waiting for the start of the school day. Snap each group to life for a few moments to establish the atmosphere in the playground.

6. Establish the convention of 'spotlighting'. The 'spotlight' in which action and sound is possible follows the character that *you* will play. As the TIR approaches each group, the group comes to life and begin to spontaneously improvise the scene.

7. Borrow a student's bag. Go to a neutral space. Step into character. You hesitate to enter the playground. Your attention is towards your pocket. You take a deep breath and enter school. As you approach the first group they come alive. The group refer to your phone. You lie about it; its cost, its origins. Perhaps your Uncle sent it from America where they're new and fashionable. Deal with each group's reaction. You may find that some show sympathy but this ordinarily breaks down into derision. The earlier groups tend to end in your walking away angrily calling, 'Call yourselves friends. I don't need you I've got other mates.' As you leave a group they must stop acting and become audience. As you move through the groups your lies become more and more implausible until finally you erupt with the truth. 'It costs £4.99 a month and my mum got it from the market with money she saved up. Just because you can afford...'. Challenge the groups' responses to you in role. You've had enough! You're not staying here to be 'shown-up'. You leave the working space... even the room!

In Part Two you have taken on the weight of the character's social disgrace. This particular piece of teacher-in-role is especially powerful and builds authority for the teacher as a fellow performer. The situation empowers the class. You have allowed the class to express some realities of their social situation in a protected way. You have revealed a set of attitudes and behaviours which now become the subject of the class' study.

Part Three: Reflective discussion, reflective drama

8. Ask the class: 'If you had to give your group's reactions a mark out of five for how close they came to reality, what number would you give it and why?' Ask each group to discuss this and come to a consensus. Each group then offers their answers and their answers are discussed. Is this

really how people might treat each other? Why? What does 'value' mean? Where do we learn what *things* (like phones or trainers) have value? Where do our reactions come from? Who influences us? You might wonder out loud, 'If we had just seen these attacks on a person because of their race, or colour or gender we would know what to call it. Discrimination towards a different race has a name – racism, or against a person because of their gender ('sex') – 'sexism'. What is the name of discrimination against a person because of their ability to 'afford the best things'? Against your level of wealth? Against being poor? Is there a name for it? Why not? Drop to the bald question: Are we worth what we own? Why does what we own matter so much? Could you imagine a world where it did not matter? Could it be any different? Is it just daft or naive to imagine that it might be?

9. Return the discussion to the dramatic situation. As the character leaves this playground how does he feel? What had he heard that upset him most? Take five again. Why were these things the most upsetting?

Group character, group mind

10. Place a volunteer in the centre of the circle. The actor creates a physical representation of the student you had previously played. The class become the character's mind. We might call the circle a 'mind trap'. We are going to try and summon a sense of the storm that's going on in his head at that moment – the thoughts that trap him in the moment. The group responds to a series of questions which you now pose: What did he hear in the playground that has stuck in his mind? What did he want to say in reply but couldn't? What is he thinking about his mother? His family? About the phone in his hand? About the people he has just met in the playground? What 'messages' has he ever heard that tell him what things are 'valuable'? The actor in the centre is invited to respond to the things that he hears. To question and challenge. In the state of mind he is put into at the end of the playground scene, what thoughts rush through his head? Tell the group: We're going to try and build that feeling, that 'mind'. Each member of the group chooses a thought, idea or statement to contribute. The circle performs the 'group mind', adding a statement one at a time as the character flits around the circle-mind in the spirit of escape. After hearing all contributions, the group might be invited to repeat their lines and the actor to react. The teacher orchestrates and raises the tone and volume. The storm rises. The character is crushed under the weight of the verbal attack.

Jump off point: small group play-making

11. The 'group mind' represents how the character felt; how he had been made to feel by the weight of the friends, the community, the world around him. You all saw him leave the school premises. Where did he go to? Home? The shops? Somewhere else? Think about how he feels. Think about what he will do. This is the story you are going to tell. In small groups develop scenes to demonstrate where his mental state leads him.

12. Insist that groups plan carefully. The initial stages of this scheme might engender an excitability which it will be necessary to manage. You may find this phase of the work needs to be slowed and made more reflective. Here are two approaches I have used: you might mark the end of a planning period by asking groups to call you over when they think they have completed the planning task and ask them to give you a full account. You might challenge their drama further during these discussions and move the group on. They have to work for your 'license to act'. Alternatively, ask groups to create their developing drama as a series of three tableaux to begin. This allows them to think clearly about a progressive narrative structure; beginning state, action, ending state. A good drama shows a person in a process of change. Once they have all achieved the tableaux and performed them, they may progress to a full rehearsal and performance.

13. Reflect together upon the scenes. What do the different possibilities show? What has he done? Stolen? Damaged himself? Taken it out on his mother? His house? Sought revenge on his friends? Put through the phone shop window? Whatever it might be, what does it tell you about who he blames for his humiliation? Who do you blame for his situation? To generate a moment of dramatic summary, you might ask each group to return to a tableau that reveals the 'centre' of their narrative . . . the most important or revealing moment. Having created this moment, invite the groups to name the moment with a title that captures the meaning of the centre. You might leave this as a usefully-tricky open task or offer more support with a proposal of a 'sentence root' that is then simply completed carefully by the group. For example, 'This is my life . . . a life of . . .' or "I burst . . . I burst with . . . at . . .'. The sentence root offers a lyrical form to the expression of the thought. Assembled together, they have a poetic form which you might like to capture as a continuous, whole-group performance poem.

In Part Three you have allowed students to enter into the dramatic situation with their own dramatic responses. These moments of 'free' exploration, where the new stages of the narrative are handed over to students, are crucial to the development of commitment. Following the performances you are ready to seize back the narrative frame.

Phase 2: Enacting the story

Part One: Story-telling

14. Before beginning the narration, explain that the story we are going to look at is a tough one; a violent one . . . but that it is rooted in truth (even if you have changed some of the details). Ask the group's permission to share the story with them. 'Is it OK if we look at the story?'

15. Ask for two volunteers: one male, one female. These two actors are going to perform the actions of the story as you tell it. One is Aaron and the other Mary. At certain points they will be given lines to perform. You will gesture to them when this is the case.

    Here is the story of Aaron and Mary:

    New York. Some say, the most violent city in the world. In the heart of New York is Central Park. Some say, the most dangerous park in the most dangerous city. Or at least, it was on the day I am going to tell you about, for one of these characters.

    It's a cold December day. Snow has fallen. Mary is standing on the corner of a busy New York street. Steam is rising from the subway vents. Mary is 14.

    When she was a child Mary had lived next door to Aaron. They had been the closest of friends. When they learned to walk they learned to walk by holding each other up. When they learned to talk they learned to talk by talking to each other. Their families were like family to each other. At 11 they went to secondary school. Everything changed. At secondary there seemed to be a problem with their friendship. Not a problem between Aaron and Mary but with everyone else. It didn't seem OK to the students in school that a boy and a girl should be best friends. Very quickly it became a problem. They worked out a strategy. At school they pretended they didn't know each other. They hung out with their other friends and stayed apart. You wouldn't think they even knew each other. But after school, every day, they would meet.

    It was at about this time that Aaron's family had to move house. Aaron's father lost his job. There were lots of redundancies. The mortgage couldn't be paid and so Aaron's family moved to a smaller house in a nearby but less prosperous part of the city.

Aaron and Mary still met each day; at a corner where two busy city streets joined; half way between their neighbourhoods.

It is here that we find Mary standing on a cold December night waiting for Aaron.

At this point ask the actor playing Mary to begin acting as you give your account.

Mary is cold. Perhaps she is stamping her feet to stay warm. She looks at her watch. It is 4.25pm. Aaron is always on time. 4.35pm. It's unlike him to leave her standing there on her own. She waits. Time passes. Traffic is passing. A yellow cab blows its horn. She looks at her watch. It is 4.40pm. She looks down the street towards Aaron's house. Nothing. She's thinking about Aaron. Maybe his mates have 'got to' him at last. They both take a lot of stick for being best mates. And he's been moody since the house move. It got worse around his birthday a couple of weeks ago. It was Mary's birthday yesterday. She looks at her watch. It's 4.45pm. A man walks towards her. He is looking at her strangely: a girl alone on this dark street. She is scared. The man looks away from her and passes. Mary's had enough. She thinks; 'I'll give him one more minute and then I'm going home.' She waits. Her watch ticks away another minute. She turns to walk home.

The actor does as you say.

As she takes the first few steps she hears footsteps approaching her from behind. She thinks about the man. This is New York. It could be a mugger with a gun. She carries on walking, looking straight ahead, terrified. The footsteps are right behind her. They slow down. She turns. It is Aaron.

The second actor now joins the scene.

Mary is relieved. She smiles. Aaron doesn't respond. He doesn't apologise or explain or even begin a conversation. He walks. His head down and his hands deep in his pocket. Mary follows him. He is walking fast, a little ahead of her. Something is wrong with him. She asks him what it is. Have his mates been getting at him? Is it his dad again? Has he had his school report? Aaron gives no answer. He just walks.

They get to the gates of the park: Central Park. Mary hasn't even been looking where they've been going. They're not allowed in the park after dark. It's dangerous. Aaron walks straight through the gates. Mary stops. She doesn't want to go in. But she doesn't want to be alone either. Not this far from home. She stops for a moment, shouting to Aaron. He stops. But he doesn't turn around. He's on the main path. It's lit with street lights. It doesn't look too dark. He's her best friend. She steps through the gates and catches him up. They carry on walking.

Mary's talking fast now. She's scared and if she keeps talking and pretending everything is normal she'll be alright. She's talking about a teacher who's bugging her; about this lad she likes; about her birthday and all the great things she got . . . about her new phone. She'd better not get it muddy . . .

They get to a fork in the path. To the left is the main pathway: brightly lit, a busy route for joggers, patrolled by police on horseback 24 hours a day. To the right a path goes off into the darkness into the trees. No lighting. No police. Aaron steps off the brightly lit path and carries on walking. Mary stops. She shouts:

Instruct the actor to repeat these lines after you.

'Aaron. Don't go down there! It's dark! Mum'll go mad if she knows we're in the park! Your dad'll . . . ' No reply from Aaron. He shrugs his shoulders. Carries on walking. 'Aaron!'

Again, Mary has a choice; to *not* follow Aaron and find herself alone in Central Park, or to follow him, her best friend, her upset best friend. She waits. And then she follows him again, running to catch up with him. Now she is very scared. She isn't talking she is walking as closely to Aaron as she can, looking from side to side into the darkness, listening for sounds. She is walking quickly. She overtakes him. She walks on a little and stops; realising that Aaron isn't following her. She stops and turns around. She takes out her phone. 'I'm calling my mum.' Aaron is standing with his head down, one hand still in his pocket. He looks up slowly. For a second he looks into her face, but then his eyes drop to her hands. He is fixed on the object in her hand . . . on her phone. He says,

'Give me yer phone.'

The actors speak these lines as you feed them in.

'What?' says Mary.

'Give me your phone!'

Mary laughs. She thinks he's joking. 'Stop it, Aaron.'

Louder: 'Give me your phone!'

She tries laughing. But the look in Aaron's eyes tells her he is not joking. 'Aaron, what's the matter?' Please. Stop it.' She's crying.

Aaron takes his other hand from his pocket. In it is his father's gun. He's picked it up from the bedside cabinet. He raises his hand. It is heavy. He brings his second hand up to help take the weight. He says again. 'Give me yer phone.'

Mary quickly tosses her new phone towards him. He keeps the gun pointed at her as he steps forward to pick it up.

Mary backs away from him, stumbling. As he stoops to pick up the phone she runs. Back up the path towards the lights. As she goes she shouts, 'I'm gonna tell me dad!'

At this Aaron raises the gun, both hands on it. He aims. He fires, misses. The bullet disappears into mud. He aims again. He fires: misses. The bullet hits a tree. He takes a stronger stance, aims slowly and carefully: fires. The bullet hits Mary in the stomach. She falls.

Aaron picks up the phone. Puts the gun back into his pocket and goes home. At home he eats his dinner. He does some homework. He watches TV. At around 8.45pm there is a knock on the door. It is the police.

Mary's wound wasn't fatal. Had he thought about what he had done, had he called an ambulance at any point within about two hours of the shooting Mary may have been saved. But he didn't. Hours after the shooting a man is walking a dog in the park. The dog runs off into the trees and won't come back. The man follows the dog and finds Mary. The shot had cut into her stomach. She had lain for two hours and slowly bled to death.

Aaron was arrested that night. He had made no attempt to hide his crime. The gun was back in his father's bedroom. Recently fired and not cleaned. He was the last person seen with her. And the phone? He had cleaned the phone, carefully removing all the mud ... And then he had put his own sim card into the phone. He couldn't even get online with *his* sim in it. He phoned two friends. Telling them about his new phone. When the police knocked on his door Mary's missing phone was in his hands; his fingers sliding across the touch-screen in a final, satisfied text. Two hours of happy texting, happy calling ... as Mary lay in the mud.

Silence.

This is a difficult story. You may worry about telling it to Year 7 students. The important thing is that in this circumstance students are given the chance to respond and explore to these 'hard facts of living' in a way which they are not with the multitude of news stories and violent narratives which sometimes seem to wallpaper our lives. We need the difficult story to gain a serious response and to warrant a serious investigation. It is important to leave time for students to articulate their private responses. The pace of the ensuing discussion will be slow; and the better for it.

Part Two: Reflection and object as character

16. Refer the class back to the 'group mind' of the earlier character. How much further would things need to go to produce an 'Aaron'? How do such things happen? How did Aaron see Mary at the moment before the shot? Did he recognise her? What was be thinking about? Was he 'obsessed' or 'fixated' on simply owning that phone? How does a phone become imbued with such value... and a person so valueless? Who is to blame? Aaron is clearly responsible... But anyone else? Who might you 'accuse'? Invite statements of 'I accuse...'. Does it make sense to accuse the phone?

17. Reveal the bag and phone used in the earlier phases. Ask the class to imagine that the phone in the bag is Mary's phone. Is this the 'object' which caused her death? Perhaps place it in a clear plastic bag so it has the look of police evidence. Now slowly take it out. Lay it in the centre of the circle. How did this object get to be so important in both Aaron's and Mary's mind? We can all see what it is... some plastic, some glass, some clever electrical circuits... but it has much more 'value' than this? Can we say why? Can we say how?

18. The 'speaking object'. Let's imagine something weird. Imagine that the phone could speak. What would it say? Imagine the phone speaking at four different moments in its 'life':

    i.   As it sat in the shop window waiting to be bought. As if it were calling out to be bought. 'Buy me...'

    ii. As it was unwrapped by Mary on her birthday. When she first saw it and was thrilled. 'You've got me now...'

    iii. As Aaron saw it in Mary's hand as they stood in the park. As if they were casting a spell on him. 'You must have me...

    iv. As it lay in a plastic bag marked with a tag as police evidence. Perhaps it is mocking them both. 'How foolish...'.

    Building out from your modelling suggestions, invite other responses to further establish the principle. The class is moved into four groups and allocated one of the above. As a group they are going to create a short monologue for the phone. This should be discussed and then noted down on paper. After the period of preparation one or more members of the group will perform their group's monologue. You might introduce the idea of some simple choral speaking so that the monologue can be spoken as a whole group.

In Part Two we have moved through reflection and philosophical investigation to a dramatic abstraction. The discussions may be tricky; the questions being asked might have a productive awkwardness about them for which there is no resolution. As ever, it is the uncovering of this depth of questioning that is of benefit and educational value. The best discussions of this nature leave the participants stretched, bewildered but desiring completion. The struggle for completion is the struggle for meaning. In this way the drama carries on into their own lives and their own private moments.

Amidst the bewilderment, we move straight to the abstraction of the anthropomorphised object. Where our capacity to articulate the meaning of the situation runs out, our imagination can continue to answer. The object-as-a-character approach is a powerful tool for making concrete meanings that we may find difficult to articulate.

We see that the object is loaded with significance in the narrative – but now, in our drama, the object becomes 'cathexed' with meaning as a theatrical object. 'Cathexis' is a term from psychoanalysis used to describe how a person might instil an object (or idea or action) with magnified significance. Bond coins the phrase to describe how on stage objects are similarly imbued with layers of meaning – perhaps by the sheer fact of its appearance on a stage, or by the uses to which it is put within the narrative. This is high-order theatre-making happening in your classroom.

Part Three: Scenes from a life: a dramatic time-line

19. Let us consider what we know about Aaron and Mary's relationship; from their early friendship to the start of secondary school. Either generate a full set of 'moments of significance' through discussion and note these down, or, use the following suggested list. Within this, there is scope for lightness – particularly in their early lives.

    i.   Mary and Aaron were born only one day apart. They first met as 'babes in arms'.

ii.   When they were first able to sit up, they sat facing each other.

iii. When they first learnt to walk, they helped each other stand.

iv.   When they went to school, they (gulp) held each other's hands.

v.   When they could, they sat next to each other in class.

vi.   In the summer holidays, their families always went on holiday together.

vii. When they went to high school, people laughed at their closeness.

viii. At high school, they learnt to pretend they didn't know each other.

ix.   They met every day after school and continued their friendship in secret.

x.   One day, Mary waited for Aaron on the street corner...

Once the list is complete, it might be useful to copy or print it onto individual strips of paper for distribution to groups. The next stage will be to create small groups (perhaps two, three or four – as appropriate to the scenes) and invite the groups to create a 'snap-shot' tableau to illustrate the scene. Each group will be allocated a space in the room such that when the tableaux are presented they will move successively and smoothly from one to the next event in a 'dramatic time-line'. You may take the role of announcing the title of each piece – as written.

20. 'Shouting from the sidelines'. You might discuss where in this time-line there is room for murder; where do those negative feelings – the jealousy, the focus on 'things' like phones, the anger – come from. What is missing? Are there external pressures away from their relationship which impact upon them? What is being 'shouted from the sidelines'? Together with your group, find a dramatic way of representing these important elements in the time-line and perform the complete sequence again.

Part Four: Small group play-making: a final straw

21. Through our discussions and abstractions we take ourselves into a much wider view of the meaning of the central actions and help to ensure that we avoid the simple naturalistic readings of the action. Now, take that deepened sensibility back into Aaron's reality; move back to a naturalistic dramatic setting. Again, it is time to release the class into their own narrative responses. Aaron was 20 minutes late to meet Mary. He was in his house. Something happened; something that was the 'tipping point' for him...the final straw. Something made him go to his parents' bedroom and get his father's gun. What could this have been? Invite the group to 'surprise' us with their answers. Who might be part of the situation? We know his father is in the house. There are other members of his family present. Recap the 'given circumstance' by taking five facts on Aaron's

home-life that have already been introduced. Restrict the scenes to the three minutes before Aaron leaves the house with the gun. It must end on his exit into the cold street. The groups prepare and move towards performance.

22. Whilst watching the scenes in performance, continue to exercise the positing of underlying questions. These are *your* questions arising from the student's creative output. The asking of the questions may be enough in itself; perhaps they are not discussed, only floated. Why does the father have a gun in the house? Is the murder, in any sense, the father's fault for keeping a gun? Who do you feel sympathy for here? What pressures are bearing down on this family? What makes Aaron snap? How has Aaron learnt what to value? What matters? Prepare to discuss America's approach to gun-control. Etc...

23. As before, you might invite groups to capture the 'centre' or central meaning, of their scenes with a complete sentence root, 'Aaron's home, a place of...where...'. As a development of this approach, perhaps these statements can this time be allocated by 'witnessing' groups rather than by the group who made each scene. For example, Group 1 creates Group 2's statement, Group 2 create for Group 3, etc...Alternatively, arrive at these statements by whole group discussion. 'What do we think this scene shows us...?

Part Five: The whole group meeting: flashing forward

24. Meet the parent. Move to a point in the story after Aaron has been imprisoned. Hot-seat Aaron's father or mother. This can be accomplished with one actor taking the part(s) or, in the form of a 'distributed hot-seat' in which the whole group answers for the character by answering the questions that you pose. It should be pointed out that they are ALL the character and that answers should 'accumulate' and avoid straight contradiction – (though without limiting the possibility of an internal struggle). Either way, students should play the character and be in control of the content. You will find it useful for your own questions to have an interrogatory or accusatory edge. Some suggestive priming questions might be: Do you feel responsible? Who do you think is responsible? We are told that you have written to the company making these phones...what did you say? Isn't this just trying to shift blame? Have you seen Mary's parents since? They were old friends. Describe the meeting. How do you feel about Aaron now? Allow the class to lead the direction of questioning.

25. At the end of the hot-seating 'remind' the parent that they are waiting outside a meeting room in a prison to discuss Aaron's future. It is now several years since the murder (perhaps bringing us into the present day). Ask them to describe the corridor they are sitting in; its look, its colour, its feel. Have they been here before? How do they feel about the place? Aaron is due to be moved to an adult prison and he has been recommended for a parole board hearing. Explain that this means that it is possible that he will be released before the end of his sentence. The authorities have called together a large group of experts, professionals and adults closely involved in the story. At the meeting that is about to take place a decision must be taken regarding Aaron's future. Should he be released? Is he still a danger?

26. Explain that we are going to try and hold that meeting here amongst us and that students are to take on the roles of people who might be there. You might like to explain the idea of Dorothy Heathcote's 'mantel of the expert'. Suggest that you play the 'chairperson of the meeting' – perhaps the prison governor – and discuss the kinds of people you would be interested in inviting. This list should be broad. Some characters might be those personally involved in the story, but you need to gather together experts and professionals who might have a specific opinion or stance to take on the question. There might be police officers, Aaron's head-teacher, his form-teacher, child psychologists, criminal psychologists, university professors with expertise on law or criminal responsibility; expanding further, you could call someone who fights for gun control (some background regarding the USA may be necessary), you could invite the chief executive of the phone manufacturers, a celeb 'sponsor' of the phone or an advertising agency. The range of experts invited will determine the range and depth of the discussion that is possible. It will be important to note that although the *surface* question is about Aaron's release, the *underlying* questions might be different. What could they be? For example, the underlying question of criminal responsibility – is Aaron solely to blame for his actions or could the finger be pointed at others? Or, 'Is it ever right to consider a criminal also as a victim?' In this way you allow the discussion to be a vehicle for drawing together ideas that have been touched upon by the scheme. The meeting then takes in a sense of summation as we approach the end of the scheme. We are asking big questions, but still within the frame of the drama.

27. Give students a short amount of time to discuss their roles together. During this time, tour the class and suggest roles where there are difficulties or (possibly) duplication. Tell students that they should prepare to introduce

themselves with their character's full name and title. They should also have a clear idea of whether they think Aaron should be released and who they think, beyond Aaron, might share responsible for Mary's death. Explain that the nature of the group in the meeting – a panel of experts and involved adults – will be very different to the nature of the group as a class. 'Take five' on how they think it will be different. Suggest that their posture and body language will be different and ask them to prepare to adopt the new characteristics. It is useful to 'count them in' to character and as you do so to progressively transform your own body language and vocal character-istics. When the group is in role introduce yourself and the purpose of the meeting. Reiterate that you believe it is impossible to discuss the case of Aaron without touching upon the much broader issues of the current state of our culture... but that the tragic story of Aaron and Mary... and Mary's family... are the driving force behind our discussion. The meeting will take a decision upon Aaron's release but will also be exploring the background to Aaron's story and trying to give Mary's family some understanding of what happened and why. You might suggest, 'We cannot understand an individual without understanding the world in which they live and has created them...'.

The participants in the meeting are then invited to introduce themselves and the discussion begins. You allow it to find its own way; challenging, asking for clarification and further information, managing the discussion by maintaining discrete 'threads' of argument, etc. as necessary.

The meeting should end with a vote on Aaron's release, though the ultimate decision will be yours. Coming out of role, ask the group to consider what decision the governor might realistically take. This is the decision that will be taken.

28. Final moment: In the interests of narrative satisfaction it is useful to think about the closing moments of the scheme carefully. Aaron is either to be released or not. He is sitting in a cell waiting for the outcome of the parole board meeting. Ask a student to try and enact a tableau of Aaron as he waits. A plain table and chair will be useful. Ask the group to try and read how he feels. Ask them to suggest other possibilities – some simple forum theatre. As the actor holds the image, other group members might step forward to 'thought-track' him. Does he want to be released? Does he feel that he deserves it? Does he accept full responsibility for Mary's death? Does he regret his actions? What will Aaron's reaction be as he is told the result of the decision taken? He might not even speak but he does react clearly.

Now either yourself or a student will enter and give the decision in very simple terms, 'Aaron, you are free to leave' or 'Aaron, it's a "no" – you must stay'. His reaction might not be something we would expect. A few students might try out this moment and offer different versions of his reaction; whatever he is told, he may weep, or say, 'No', or he may give a look of terror or he may smile...

29. With your final volunteer in place, narrate the final moment.

The guard who came in to give Aaron the news broke a rule. S/he is a guard who has got to know Aaron well over the years and even looks on him with some sympathy. After giving the news, s/he says, 'I'll leave you for a few moments to think about the decision.' And as s/he walks away s/he places something on the table. Something s/he thinks will be helpful to him. Something he can use to speak to someone about the decision...maybe his parents. The guard places a mobile phone on the table and leaves the room. Aaron looks at the mobile. Final possible questions are left hanging:

'What does Aaron do with the phone?' Step away from it in fear, smash it, simply use it, etc?

or

'What does Aaron hear the phone say to him now?'

The End.

Year 7/8 scheme: *Miguel and the aliens*

> This has always been a very popular scheme of work with young people. From its initial hook in the question of extra-terrestrial life, through the story of 'simple' abductee Miguel, to its shift into free-wheeling situation comedy, this is a scheme which asks questions around belief, scepticism, science, responsibility, tolerance, diversity and dramatic structure.

Phase 1: Setting the scene

Part One: Aliens game

1. This game is useful not only because it is an active and compelling introduction of the theme, but also, because the narrative contained within the story posits the idea of a threatening alien power. The game starts in hostility to the 'alien race' and goes on to subvert this initial fearfulness into comic domesticity. The playing of the game is quite straightforward, but I hope that the description of it won't become too laboured here. The game format is similar to other games that you might recognise as the description continues. After asking whether the class would like to play a game (of course they would!), invite the group to stand in a circle. Mime the placing of a heavy box in the centre. Begin your explanation in mode as a tongue-in-cheek story-teller.

   This is a game that involves the release of a dangerous creature into the room. It is currently captured within this sealed, shiny, steel, refrigerated, highly-secure box. It is a creature from another world, a world dangerous to human beings. Do you want me to open the box? (Of course they do!) First let me warn you. This creature (who some of you might know from films in the Alien *series) has one problem that threatens its very survival – it has no womb. (This is going to get a little gruesome!) Instead, it has to find a 'host' species to grow its young; it is a 'parasite' – it lives off* *another creature – and that creature is us: human beings. Here's what happens. In its 'reproductive form' the creature is only the size of a football but it has powerful, muscular **flaps** with which it can propel... or launch... itself around the room. Its single task... its purpose in being alive... is to reproduce. It will do so by (wait for it...) impregnating you with its tiny, alien egg. (Demonstrate this as you continue.) It will attach itself with its strong 'suckers' to you face... and its finger-length proboscis will slide itself down your throat and gently drop its egg into your stomach. There, it will begin to grow, using your stomach as its warm, safe womby chamber, until the day it is ready to be born... and then... it won't climb back up your throat, cough itself up and fly away with a nice, 'Thanks, mummy, bye bye'. No, when it is ready to be born... it will rip its way out of your stomach by the shortest route... straight out... (with a scream) WwwwAAAA!*

You might find yourself and the group having a good old nervous laugh about this. You might wonder out loud, 'I wonder why aliens are always so dangerous?' Then return to the game.

*Do you still want to open the box? (Of course they do!) When it is released it will instantly begin throwing itself around the room. It will come for you. When it sticks upon your face you will have about three seconds to get rid of it before it drops its little egg... Now, the game works like this... if the alien is stuck on my face (put both hands over your face to show you have it) I will have to pull it off (it makes a very sucky kind of noise like this...) and pass it to someone else on the other side of the circle and shout their name. They must immediately catch it and cover their face with their hands. Now, here's the tricky bit... if it sticks on **my** face, its muscley wings will stick on the face of THIS person on my right and they must cover their face on that side with the hand closest to me, similarly, the person on my left hand side must do the same with their closest hand. If a person doesn't react quickly enough – or if they cover their face with the wrong hand, they are out and must sit down. People who are **out** must remain in the circle and gently make the creature's 'sucky' sound. The alien's wing will continue to stick on the NEXT person's face, even if there are people out in between.*

2.   We suggest that you play the game through a few times without the penalty of being out, in order to fully establish the rules with everyone. When the game is in full swing it can be a fast and raucous competition that takes concentration and is highly enjoyable. To start the game *for real*, remind the group of the steel box; return to the story-telling mode. Ask finally, if they really want to release the alien (of course they do) and approach the box with trepidation. Mime the release of secure catches – which might hiss as you release each one – and then lift the lid with a final long hiss. Take the creature out at arms length, return to your own place in the circle...add the noise of its malevolent suck and throw it...calling someone's name as you do so...the deadly game has begun!

Part Two: Discussion

3.   As the game concludes with two winners (it doesn't make sense after two...it doesn't make much sense after three, as you'll see) move quickly on into discussion. How would we describe that particular creature? It isn't a real creature...it was imagined by someone. Why did they imagine such a terrible and dangerous alien? Why not a nice friendly one? (It'd be a boring game of course!) Perhaps sometimes, we just enjoy the drama of the dangerous. What does 'alien' mean? It really means, 'not from here' or 'from another place'. We do have an idea of 'an illegal alien' – meaning someone in a country who shouldn't be there. It means the same as 'illegal immigrant'. So let's talk about aliens from outer space. Do you believe in them? Is there evidence of them? Does anyone have any experience of them or know someone who does...or know any stories of people who have stories to tell?

4.   Share these stories respectfully but also don't thwart scepticism too heavily – we will need it for the next stage. You might also discuss why aliens might come here to Earth; to study us, (why?), to prepare for invasion, do they need our help? How would you feel about someone who claims to have been abducted? What would you suspect about them? That they were a liar? A fraud? An attention seeker? Mad? Why might you think these things? Why would you NOT want to believe them? Is it good or useful to be so 'sceptical'? Etc. As the discussion begins to run its course, ask the class whether they would like to meet someone who really claims to have been abducted by aliens. Of course they would.

Phase 2: Enacting the story

Part One: Miguel (teacher-in-role)

5. Explain firstly, that he (or she) is very shy. Only a few months ago, he was a poor peasant farmer living on a field no bigger than this room, on the edge of a desert, working every day to grow beans for sale in the town. The only income for his wife and family. Now he tours the world, speaking about his experience aboard the alien ship. It is the fact that he was such a 'simple' man, without electricity or television, who had never been to a cinema – without any real experience of the modern world – that makes people want to believe him. But some are not so sure ... his storytelling has made him famous ... and perhaps rich ... Would they like to meet him? They will have to look after him and treat him gently.

6. Now explain that *you* are going to play the farmer, Miguel, yourself. You might leave the room or simply turn around. The character you present will be vulnerable, out of place and out of his depth – but there is something about him that suggests an underlying strength. Is he deceiving us with his 'fake simple peasant act'? You have sowed the seeds of this scepticism earlier. You might even try a soft Hispanic accent and show him struggling for the English words. Of course, you are welcome to invent your own abduction story. Ours is general enough to be recognisable; it is stitched together from widely-known similar reported experiences that are all over the web. The bare bones of Miguel's story are:

> *He lives in a 'shack' with his wife and small family. It is hard land to farm. His hands are raw and bloody. His back bent and humped. He grows hard beans. It is all that will grow there. He has a well for water and a single room. There is no electricity. He avoids the city. Sometimes, at a great distance, across the flat landscape he has seen planes pass by in the air.*
>
> *One day he was out in his field, with his head down breaking up the dry soil. He saw something in the empty blue sky – another plane? He put his head back to the ground. Looking up again, he saw that the dot in the air had got much bigger, it had come closer. He watched it for a few seconds ... then carried on his work. Moments later, the craft had come right above him. He was in its bright shadow. It was so large that he couldn't see the edge. He dropped his tools and tried to run ... but found he couldn't*

Then a blinding light flashed and he found himself on the space ship, surrounded by 'aliens'.

They read his mind and were able to speak to him in his own language (Spanish). They conducted experiments on him. Some of them involved exploring his body... and some of them... his mind and memory. They gave him good-tasting – mush – to eat that was perfect for him and improved his health. They helped him; his hands were smooth and clean and his back straightened.

After what felt like months out of the Earth's orbit – flying around the universe, Miguel was dropped back exactly where he had been taken from. At first, he couldn't remember what had happened to him. He returned home and his wife and children were shocked to see him... he had been gone for a full month... And couldn't say why. They thought he had been taken by bandits... or had run away to the city.

Slowly, his memory returned and he was able to speak of what had happened to him.

7.   Now invite questions. The group might want to know what the aliens looked like. What the experiments were? How he got to be famous? Whether he is lying? Etc.

   Finally, perhaps out of irritation at their doubting of him, Miguel will leave. He might be shaken or angered by the group's hostility. He will give some subtle indications that he may be lying... Does he now have a nice house with a pool and HD telly?!

   Once the character has 'left the room' discuss the group's responses to him. Do we believe him? Why not? Is there anything he could say or show you to make you believe him? Why are we so sceptical? Is it healthy to be so?

Part Two: Quick, one-minute improvisation

8.   As a way of quickly shifting the focus away from the whole group work and to distribute our experience of the main character, invite the group to try and 'realise' Miguel's return home. This will involve small groups (three or four) with Miguel, his wife, his child/children and perhaps one other person who the group can choose, e.g. a neighbour, friend of Miguel, relative of his wife. The small groups should work quickly to create *just* the moment that Miguel walks back onto the farm – or into the shack. Does he walk in as if nothing has happened? Is he bewildered and staggering? Is he staring at

his perfect hands? Stretching his straight back? Does he remember anything? Is his wife angry? Scared? Groups must only make a one-minute scene but must pack into it everything the audience will need to understand the situation. There might be silence and the words you choose must be chosen with great care.

Part Three: Aliens and their science

9. Invite the group to assume – for the purposes of our drama – that Miguel is telling the truth. If it isn't restricting the group's freedom to imagine too much, you might show the striking image of the human surrounded by small aliens from the film, 'Close Encounters of the Third Kind'. (Of course, explaining that it is an image from a film and not Miguel's holiday snaps!)

    So, what experiments might the aliens have conducted? They are scientists. What do they want to discover about us? Remember, they experimented on his body, but also his mind. If they needed to experiment, does that mean that they have very different bodies and minds? In order to make this work, we will first have to 'invent' the aliens. This might be in two stages:

Stage one:

Create new and perhaps large groups. In a discussion, each group has to come up with a set of contrasts that tell us about the aliens compared to humans. For example, 'Humans grow hair on their head, aliens have no hair', 'Humans have one heart in their chest, aliens have three hearts around their body' etc. You might suggest that these 'contrast points' include not only bodies but the mind and society. E.g. 'Humans normally live in family groups, aliens have no family groups', etc. Perhaps every group can offer three contrast points. Then share your ideas. This process helps to give a whole group, shared understanding of alien life.

Stage two:

Taking elements that have been revealed in the above, we are now going to try and 'physicalise' the aliens. Invite the group onto their feet. Perhaps find some appropriate 'alien music' online to create tension and atmosphere. Explain that if we are going to try and enter the aliens' world and act as if we were them, we will need to know how we might do that. So, let's find our 'inner alien'(!) The group moves around the room and experiments with their own bodies; their posture, gait, stance, step, etc as you feed in information from the contrast points and watch for good practice, freezing and sharing this as you go to build a group consensus on the alien. You might go further and look for the alien's voice; or are they silent? Once established across the group, ask how they might greet each other, how they tell each other apart, whether some are more important than others and how they show this?

Stage three:

Having created and experienced alien life, we are now ready to return to Miguel and the experiments that were conducted on him. What was this alien science mission's task? What technology do they have? To look inside our body, would they need to cut it? How would they read our memories? Is there machinery involved? What noises does the machinery make? Ask the group to add their own questions to your list. Suggest that we imagine our own alien science.

This is the space craft. There are many rooms within it. What colour are the walls? What lights the room? If you touched the walls, how would they feel? Can you tell what they are made of? You are the alien scientists with your own unique experiments to conduct. In each room you all know how your experiment works, how the machines work, what buttons to press and what leavers to pull. You all know what sounds each machine makes in its various phases of operation. We will hear these sounds during your experiment.

Now, with your alien music playing in the background, invite the groups to create their experiments. They must decide what the experiment is designed to find out and make this into a simple statement that will introduce each 'performance'. 'An experiment to find out, for example, how human beings digest the food they put in their mouths. They must invent and mime the equipment required and how it works. Each person should know what their own individual task is within the experiment. Everyone might have a slightly different role in the work. Of course, one of them will be Miguel in each group and have the experiment done to them. How does he feel about that? Does he want to run, complain... or is he willing... or scared? The aliens might speak as they work... But what we want to see is the action of the complicated experiment. It's a movement piece accompanied by the alien music. Give the groups time to think and prepare and view the experiments in each room of the craft.

10. A 'thought-bomb' to seed in passing: Looking at the aliens we have created, perhaps they aren't so different to us. I wonder if it's possible that these are not aliens from another planet but human beings from far into the future? Could they be what we evolve into in a million years? Could they have travelled across time instead of space?

Part Four: The report

11. What did you find out about humans through your experiments? Every week the science ship has to make a report back to their home planet with all that has been learnt this week. It's an important time...you will be reporting to the leaders of the planet; to the 'Council'. They need to know what you have discovered (time may be running out). Explain that the group is going to improvise this reporting back scene. Set the room, using lighting if you have it available, to make two distinct areas. The first, the 'communication room' of the space ship near Earth and the second, the council chamber back on their home planet.

    You are going to play the "chairperson" of the Council and everyone else, except for the reporting scientists, the Council members. The scientists take it in turns to make their report.

12. Now the 'game element' in this sequence is for the Council *not* to understand the new facts that are reported to them about human beings. They will be *purposefully* obtuse and force the scientists to try and explain very simple facets of human life. The council members might even find the descriptions of human life hilarious, but they will also try to understand. You can expect the reporting scientists to become increasingly frustrated, and you might need to put a time limit on each group's report.

13. At the end of the sequence, discuss what the aliens' questions reveal about their own life and civilisation. What sort of place is it to live? Would you like it? Is it fairer? Does it have families? Leaders? Schools? Money? Do individuals *own* things like we might? Are there countries? Who might fight against each other? Does it control its own weather? Are there different countries, religions, races?

Part Five: Discussion and revelation: why did the aliens come?

14. So, why is it urgent for the aliens to come here and to study human life so closely? It could be pure science...just to learn about things to increase their knowledge. But it might be something else. What might it be? Discuss.

It turns out that when Miguel came back to the Earth, and began to remember his experience, he also found about his person...in a forgotten pocket perhaps...a letter. A letter addressed to 'The Leaders of the Peoples of Earth'. It was in a special container, written on strange paper in glowing ink. (You have such a piece of paper and produce it now!) You might drop back into character as Miguel to give the following account.

He (or I) found the strange letter in a deep pocket. He saw how it was addressed and didn't know what to do with it. (What would you do with it? Who is the leader of the peoples of the Earth? Discuss.) He knew he had to deliver it...and began the long walk to the city. On the road, racing across the dry desert, he was met by a fleet of cars, with flags of many nations flying on their roofs. They stopped when they saw him and asked for the letter. It seems they had been expecting it.

Here is what the letter said: (you might now speak as the Alien Council Chamber Leader) 'Fine people of Earth. We contact you from a world beyond you in time and space. We have been studying you. Watching you for many hundreds of your years. We say, "O brave, new world,that has such people on it". We wish to be your friends...and we ask for your help.

As clever as you might think we are, we have been very foolish. We have not taken care of our own home planet – its delicate balances – and our planet is dying. It is too late for us to do anything to save it. We have searched the universe for a place we can call home...a place that can support our life-form...a place with the correct balance of what you call oxygen and hydrogen and the other gases. In the vastness of all space, there is only one place where we can live: your Earth.

Our days are numbered and falling fast. We ask your permission to leave our own planet and to come to you, to live amongst you. We are a strong and advanced civilisation with much to offer to you. If you do not welcome us to the Earth...our species will die...and be wiped from the face of the universe for ever. Please help us. Our future is in your hands.'

15. Immediately discuss this situation. What are the implications, the dangers, the opportunities, the threats, the options? If this were to really happen, who would take the decision? How would they decide? Who would they want to take advice from?

Part Six: The human race decides

16. We move now into a new format; a complex 'mantel of the expert' scenario in which an invigorated United Nations must decide. This is a crucial decision in human history. Each person must take on a role with a very clear position or stance. Who might have something to say on this? Leaders of countries, military leaders, business leaders, people at a local level such as head-teachers of schools, experts on population growth, leaders from poorer countries, trade unionists, housing experts, food experts, etc. Encourage a wide discussion on the issues before asking students to decide upon their own character's stance. Would human beings have a duty to help the aliens? Can our planet sustain a huge influx of aliens? How many are there? How might their advanced technologies help us? How might their arrival make our lives better?

    Once discussed in general terms, invite the group to discuss and then decide upon their characters for the meeting. They might make simple name badges. Perhaps Miguel is present. You will probably chair the meeting and make an opening statement about the importance . . . for all of humankind . . . and all history . . . of the decision. 'Never, has the human race been faced with such a decision. Our future depends upon it . . . and that of an alien people . . . who some might even dare to call "Brothers and Sisters in Life."'

    The meeting begins. Allow it to flow.

    Ultimately, for a variety of reasons that might emerge (responsibility, fear perhaps), the meeting will decide to allow the alien people to come. Your expert chairing of the meeting will see to it. Perhaps you have an overriding vote (for dramatic purposes!) The meeting should end with a message written carefully by the whole group . . . maybe with conditions. To inform the alien people that they have permission to come to the Earth. Maybe Miguel (a student now in role) might speak the reply.

Part Seven: Arrival on Earth: the first meeting

17. Consider what preparations might be made for the arrival of 'the others'. You can't keep calling them 'the aliens' – give them the dignity of a name. What is the name of their planet? The name of their 'people'? Agree on this together.

    Can you imagine seeing such a strange creature for the very first time? How would you feel? Of course, we would look as strange and 'alien' as they do to us.

Split the group into two and have the two halves stand in parallel lines with their back to each other. Speak them into their roles and the situation; they are about to meet 'the others for the first time. Be careful not to tell the groups which is human and which is from the other planet. They are *both* alien to each other. Talk them into their first meeting; will 'the other' terrify you, interest you, amuse you? Will you warm to them? Be repelled by them? Do you think you will ever get used to them? Could you ever be friends with 'the other'?

Ask the groups to turn around but close their eyes. Ask them how they feel when they are about to meet 'the other'... volunteers raise their hands and we listen to their ideas. Ask them what they expect to see... pointing out that they might be an earthling or from the other planet... that's up to them. Play the alien music softly in the background and invite them all to open their eyes. There is likely to be laughter. Take all reactions seriously from within the drama: 'Why are we laughing?' Nerves? Fear? Are they so ridiculous to look at? The creature you are looking at might not understand your laughter... they might not be insulted or hurt by it. They might enjoy it... and find you just as funny. But that moment passes and you cross the space that stands between you. (Indicate for these things to happen as you narrate.) As you do so, you look into each others' faces. What you see might not be life like your own, not human or alien. But she/he looks back at you. In some way you recognise each other, you recognise life. Do you shake hands? Freeze.

Come out of that moment and talk it through.

Part Eight: The aliens next door: a leap into situation comedy!

18. Explain that you are going to make a dramatic leap. The first jump will be into the future: the 'aliens' have arrived. They are in our schools, our neighbours, our dentists, working in our shops and besides us in our offices; everything has changed. The second jump is into a different kind of drama. We've gone so far in this story... in a particular style of drama. We are going to continue and complete the story in a different 'drama genre' – one that you might all know about: situation comedy or sitcom. Discuss what the group understand by this. What sitcoms might they know about? This will be a discussion clearly related to your time and place and the examples that come forward, and that you might give, will be local to you and your group. It might be worth noting that the global phenomena of *The Simpsons* is a special kind of sitcom, as is Mr Bean – both of which you

might find useful to refer to. Discuss with the group some characteristics of a sitcom. For the purposes of the coming task you might like to settle on the following 'rules' of a sitcom:

- It is a comedy.
- There is a small group of different and easily recognisable characters. The main characters are the same each episode but other characters might come and go depending on the story for each episode.
- The comedy comes about because of the situation the characters are in.
- The situation could be described as a 'task' that one or all of the characters want to accomplish.
- The task will be interrupted in comic ways because of the limitations of the characters.
- In our situation comedy, the basic situation will be that 'aliens' have come to live next door to you or amongst you and in each episode there will be a different task that the alien or human 'family' will want to achieve.
- The task will be interrupted in comic ways because of the misunderstandings, limitations, special powers etc of the 'aliens'. It might be like the kind of comedy that is sometimes called, 'the fish out of water' comedy; the comedy comes about through someone not fitting in to the situation or place they find themselves in.
- Having checked understanding, invite the creation of new groups and suggest the following process of development for the 'sitcoms'.
- Create a 'character group'; each person should be distinctive and funny in their own right. The 'aliens' should also be particular kinds of people. You might think about describing each character in a pair of contrasting adjectives; for example, you might say Lisa Simpson is 'bright but stubborn'.
- Decide on a 'task' to be accomplished: e.g. take your alien shopping, to school, to the cinema, to get a job, etc.
- Imagine what might happen to interrupt the accomplishment of the task – how might it all go wrong?
- Suggest that groups tell the story in five steps:
  i.   Introduce the task.
  ii. Begin to achieve it and the first thing goes wrong.
  iii. Then the second – which is worse.
  iv. Then the final straw – the third problem – which is huge.
  v.   Then find a way of getting out of the fix, with the task accomplished in a surprising way or given up. Everything's alright in the end!

Groups create and rehearse their short alien sitcoms and prepare to perform them.

19. After the performance, discuss the dramas: how did it feel to be following a pattern – a 'narrative structure'. Explain that this is how much popular drama is developed. Explore why this might be the case. Also, talk about the aliens again. Do the dramas show anything interesting about how people deal with 'the unknown', 'the other'? Think about how the journey you've had regarding aliens has developed: the game with the terrifying, parasite alien, the abduction with the 'alien unknown', becoming familiar… and perhaps respectful with their different form of life, choosing to accept them, making them a part of our ordinary lives; a journey from fear to familiarity. Do you think we are generally fearful of things or people that are unfamiliar to us?

Part Nine: Final twist: the aliens' secret

20. To get us out of the scheme, return to the tone and feel of the earlier, pre-comedy line of narrative. Your might adopt the tone of the 'Alien Council Chamber Leader' again, or read her final message on paper in role as our friend Miguel:

> *This is my final message to you. I will be staying on the home planet. I am too old to make the difficult journey…I must thank you for your kindness in accepting our people into your world and into your lives. But before I end, you should know this…the journey we have made is not across the vast distances of space…it has been the more difficult journey…through the impossibilities of **time**. We, the 'alien people' are you – the human race – in 200 thousand more years of evolution…you will become us in time. When you chose to save US, you chose to save yourselves.*

The End.

This scheme has hopefully been a rich and shifting series of events which poses some significant questions along the way. The challenges seem to come thick and fast. There is both a playfulness and deadly seriousness that it is hoped you and your groups will find compelling. Your science department might like to know how you are incorporating elements of scientific method into your drama lessons.

Year 8 scheme: *Piccadilly*

Exploring the issue of homelessness has perhaps become a drama cliché; it has an element of the soap operatic within it waiting to burst out. It's important, however, to avoid the easy naturalistic family crisis scenario and to look plainly in the face – with analysis – of an important social issue. In this scheme we create opportunities for discussion of poverty, deprivation and social justice.

We have called it Piccadilly, because of its origins on the edge of inner city Manchester. Piccadilly is a public area – an open square and a bus station – that would be familiar to the classes with whom the scheme originated. Of course, you will tailor the narrative to your own situation and site the events in as familiar a setting as you can find.

Phase 1: Setting the scene

Part One: Story-telling and enacting

1. The class is seated in a half circle to create a performance space. A large pile of clothes are placed on the edge of the stage, including a large carrier bag. The teacher begins to relate an event from their own recent history (it was true once, for me). The teacher acts out the event as she/he narrates the action. Here it is. You are, of course, free to tailor, embellish and make the story your own.

    I was out late last weekend in Manchester. I went to see a film. I was with some other people who decided to get a taxi home – I was going a different direction, so, I went to Piccadilly Gardens for a bus. It was after midnight. The buses are due once an hour. I'd just missed one. I was standing on my own. It was raining. Some drunk lads passed me singing and shouting. I stepped closer to the buildings. I waited. Looked at my watch. I really wanted to be at home, in my warm, centrally-heated house. I'd sit down, probably make a piece of toast, a cup of tea; before climbing into my lovely bed. I wanted to be in my bed so much! I waited; looked at my watch. Some other people passed. We ignored each other. I looked at my watch. (Quiet.) Suddenly, out of the corner of my eye I noticed a pile of clothes. (See it.) I looked again; then away. The bus station was quiet. A bus went by empty. Engine roaring in the quiet night. I looked at my watch. (Quiet.) I looked again at the pile of clothes. I wondered where it might have come from. It was a big pile. Maybe someone's suitcase had burst and they'd not had time to pick it up. Maybe it'd been stolen and then dumped. I looked at it. There was something strange about it. Was it moving? Maybe a rat had hidden in the pile. Yes, it was moving. (Go to the pile and show how it was moving by putting your hand under it.) It was rising and falling like someone breathing. (Go back to where you were waiting.) I watched the pile . . . at a safe distance. I realised it wasn't a pile of clothes. There was somebody under the clothes. I watched. A few more people passed. I looked at my watch. I wanted my bus to come. I wanted to be safe at home. I wanted my bed! (Wait.) Then the pile moved again, more than before. A head appeared from underneath the clothes: eyes blinking. A kid about 11 or 12, but small, looked around the bus station. And then looked at me. Waiting to go home. The child stood; seemed scared of me looking at them. Was I staring? I was embarrassed now. The child suppressed a tired yawn. Strange, I couldn't tell if it was a boy or girl. They had so many layers of clothes on. Their face was so hidden. (Go over and carry out the child's actions) When they had got to their feet they took a bag from the pile of clothes and began stuffing the clothes into it. Still looking at me. Scared. Threatening. When all the clothes were in the bag, they looked around. Checking. Then walked towards me . . . as if they would stop to speak . . . then changed their mind . . . gave me one last look and passed by. Walked around the corner of the Piccadilly Hotel and disappeared. It was still raining. I looked at my watch. My bus arrived.

2. You now step out of the situation and continue: 'At least five people passed me at the bus station. Thinking back, I think most of them recognised the pile of clothes as a person. What do you think they were thinking to themselves, or saying to each other as they passed this homeless person (they probably couldn't tell it was a kid)? Firstly, what were they saying to each other about the "tramp"? Now, put the pile of clothes back and allow

a small number of volunteers to improvise passing the pile of clothes. In this way, you will gather a broad selection of attitudes towards the homeless; sympathetic or otherwise; the dramatic dialogue has begun. It might be useful to discuss with the group how these characters in the story have come to have these opinions. Where did they learn them? What might there be in their own lives that explains or supports their thinking? For example, someone might hate their low-paid job but have to work very hard over long hours to support their family... they might feel that the homeless are just unwilling to work hard.

After several people have shown us their 'characters' – invite all or some of them back onto the stage to take up a position which shows their attitude to the still hidden person in the pile of clothes (they don't know it's a child – is that significant?) You might invite an actor to take up the role of the homeless child to complete the picture. So now we have a stage picture of poverty and attitudes to it.

Ask the audience to look at each person and imagine their thoughts, backgrounds, lives. Explain that you are going to try a 'chain-tracking' exercise. This is like 'thought-tracking' in which you might touch a frozen character on the shoulder and speak their thoughts. Here, audience members will come forward, touch a character's shoulder and speak for them. They will then stay on stage and a second (then third, fourth, etc) person will come and link to the first person's shoulder and add to their comment. The 'chain-track' speech from each character should start with the original thought suggested, but might end up having five or six additional lines. It will be a simply-constructed monologue.

At the end of this process, you might think about changing the order of the people in each chain to make their 'monologue' make as much sense as possible. This is akin to the writer's editing process when creating text or narrative. You might finally hear all of the character speeches together – perhaps making audio recordings of them for later reference or evidencing purposes.

Part Two: Discussion

3. Spend a short time after the final 'enactments of attitude' summarising the attitudes demonstrated; is there sympathy, anger, embarrassment? Use a 'sentence root' to encourage formal summarising of each character: for example, 'The... (adjective) homeless... (description of action)' as in, 'The lazy homeless, wallowing in their own self-pity' (or, more simply) 'The lazy homeless, feeling sorry for themselves'.

After gathering all responses, open a discussion about the group's own and societies' attitudes towards the homeless and the poor. Why are there poor people? Why are there homeless people on our streets? Are there just not enough houses to go around? Are our feelings about it the same as any of the characters in the scene? Where do we get our ideas and feelings from? Is the existence of homeless or poor people inevitable? Is there anything that could be done about it?

Wherever the natural break comes in your lesson series, you might ask the group to find out some simple facts about homelessness and poverty – in this country and elsewhere.

Part Three: Giving a voice

4.   Ask the group: How would you lie on a cold, hard floor, covering yourself in blankets, to stay as warm and comfortable as you could? In this sequence, it might be very useful to darken the room. Invite the group to find themselves an individual spot on the floor. This is where they will lie. Explain that you are going to ask a series of questions, but you don't yet need an answer spoken out loud. 'Just prepare the answers in your head – prepare them as this homeless young person.'

> *Look around the room. This is your empty bus-station – your home for the night. Why did you choose to sleep here? More public, more safe? Look for the best spot; it is a little away from where you are now stood. Look around for the spot... and decide. Why did you choose THIS spot? Is it close to a wall? A bench? A warm air vent from a building? What is the best spot? You have bags in your hand... you are going to walk to the spot and prepare to lie down in it. How will you prepare the ground? You have a bag of clothes... where did you get them from? I am just going to watch now... some sounds or music might play in the background... really, to fill the silence... because there is nothing to say. You are on your own. The most important thing you will do tonight... is to build this cold bed of unwanted clothes with the greatest of care; to keep out the cold, the draft, the prying eyes, the rooting dog and the hungry rat. Your plan, if you can, is to disappear under this pile of clothes; to be invisible. As you work on your bed, keep an eye open for drunks, bus station cleaners, the police, the unwanted stranger... But work.*

Now stop your lead-in narration and allow the group to become absorbed in the making of their beds. You might use sound to enhance the moment:

a sound effect of a bus station, or a heavy bus engine ticking over, or pensive music, or perhaps look-up the track, 'Jesus blood never failed me yet' by Gavin Bryars, featuring an unknown homeless man. You might enhance the task by offering a set of clothes or material to each person (a lot of clothes), or more practically, allow the students to prepare in mime, up to the point where they settle down to sleep . . . and as they do so, cover them over yourself with a piece of simple cloth . . . so that finally the room is full of shapes hidden under cloth.

As they work on their beds, you might invite them to speak softly to themselves. You might feel it appropriate to ask questions that they do now answer out loud. Then again, you might find that less really is more. Let them become absorbed and try to focus on the details of their task and to settle into *living through* the experience and identifying with the character.

When everyone is settled 'for the night', you might just let them rest. Finally saying, 'We'll leave it there' and perhaps bringing them out of role and sitting quietly to reflect on that experience and their possible identification with the child.

In this opening phase you have gained commitment to the story and the character and begun to express attitudes towards the homeless and poverty. You have also opened up thinking about the sources of social beliefs; beliefs about people. In doing so you are asking students to explore their own values and beginning to develop their role as the centre of their own meaning-making, thus giving them new authority over their own thinking.

In the dramatic exploration that follows we are going to build the character of the child and create their story. In so doing we are recognising his/her humanity in a way we may have not done when we did not even recognise the pile as a person; knowing the character's narrative deepens our response and our understanding and perhaps influences our attitudes towards them.

We have chosen to make the central character a child in order to foster a deeper identification with students. You might choose to make the character older or even much older. Their age will determine the story that is now built.

Phase 2: Enacting the drama

Part One: Play-making pairs: 'Said and not said'

5. To begin the process of 'humanising' the anonymous character we begin by giving them a voice and a social 'reality' – we are 'building out' from the

original incident. We are going to imagine a scene that never happened. Imagine that instead of standing there and trying not to look at the child I had spoken to him/her. What might I have said? 'Take five*' possibilities from the class. Imagine the child spoke back. What might they have said? Again, 'take five'.

(*Note: By 'taking five' you are checking understanding, modelling responses and making material available to any groups who may find the task more challenging.)

6. Discuss the idea of public and private thought. 'Do you think we always speak exactly what we are thinking? Are we always honest in this way? Why not? There might be good reasons for not always being honest. In our drama, however, we have the chance to show not only what a person *says* but also what they *think but don't say*. What sort of conversation might the child and I have had? In pairs students are invited to create this scene. It will involve both what is said and what is not said. Each pair will have to decide how to let the audience know whether a line is a public or private thought. How will they do this? You might propose the convention of looking at the audience to show a private thought; as in an 'aside'.

    You may wish to restrict the scene to a small number of exchanges: three lines and three asides, perhaps. Such brevity requires focus and clarity and careful selection of words. In a large class the sheer number of pairs created can also be an issue, in which case, restricting the length or number of exchanges can be very helpful.

    We have set the scene and situation and now students 'jump off' into their own creations.

    Support the development of the scenes as necessary and work towards performance.

7. Discuss: What do the scenes tell us? What's the world like where this scene is possible? How do these people feel about each other? How do they feel about themselves? Dramatise the discussion: Ask for two actors to repeat the tableau of the teacher and the child in the bus station. Members of the group are invited to 'thought-track' the characters and complete the sentence formulae; 'I'm looking at you and I feel ...' and 'I see my reflection in the shop window and I feel ...'.

Part Two: Hot-seating teacher-in-role

8. Explain to the group: We are going to look closely at the child you met. Explain that you are going to take on the role of the child yourself for the

moment. It will be the class' task to treat the child carefully and try to find out as much as they can about him. You take on the role; you cling to the bag of clothes on your knee. You are hard to talk to. The students have to be very gentle with you or you threaten to walk out. You challenge them in role: 'I thought you wanted to know...'. In answering their questions you are 'cagey' and non-specific about the details of your story. This is a difficult experience for you. You are careful to leave the answers 'open'. Why did you leave? Point to your family...but explicitly exclude the obvious soap operatic version of family strife (drunken father, drugs, etc.) Maybe your father was a figure of relatively high social status: a teacher or businessman? Make them really struggle for a narrative. Confound their ideas. Give them a problem to work on. Of course, you will have to have a clear story in mind so that your answers are tied to a central spine of truthfulness – but don't let *your* story become theirs. Move on to focus on the realities of the street; how people treat you, how you see other people. Don't be sentimental – be precise in your detailing. Hint at anger. Get to a point where you begin to talk about your last day in the family home. Then stop and come out of role. This should have been an infuriating and disconcerting experience for the group. You have modelled attitudes and emotions and suggested tensions and difficulties, but the child's situation is strongly out of focus. It is this need for clarity which will drive the ensuing dramatic explorations. You have opened an imaginative gap, which needs to be filled.

Part Three: The object: the door

9. The child has just led us to the moment that they left their house for the last time. We are going to explore their last few moments in the house, but we are going to build up to it very carefully. At that moment the child must have walked through a door: maybe closing it behind themselves, or leaving it open to avoid waking people. If we can get a clear picture of what this door *was* we will understand a lot about their life. It's a tiny detail which tells us much. Now draw the door frame in the air and invite students to imagine the door which fills this gap. The class close their eyes and try to visualise it clearly. When they have a clear picture, they raise their hands and you choose a selection of people to describe the door. You question them in detail. Start with the physical details; colour, condition, construction, materials. You might go on to ask them to tell you what this door 'means'. Offer a sentence formula: If you were going into the house through this

door you might say, 'This is a door into...'. Take as many offers of description as you wish. Some students might not be able to 'visualise' the door but could give you a clear list of characteristics (this would be my approach), some might need to act through walking towards and through the door. Make all responses valid and suggest that this might relate to differences in how we see/learn/understand things.

10. Move to the placing of the door into the child's story. You have created the door. Now show us how the child walked through this door for the last time. Is it night and they are sneaking out silently? Do they storm out and slam it? Do they walk out without knowing that they will not return? Do they walk through it as they do every day? Anything is possible. Invite a real range of possibilities; opening up the narratives that are to come. Ask the group to think for a few moments and then ask for volunteers to enact their own version of the departure.

Part Four: Small-group play-making: the last home

11. The class is now going to dramatise this character's last five minutes in the family home. Create mixed-sex groups of any number (not too large). As a first step, ask for all characters to be in the position that they end up in when the child walks out (i.e. the final tableaux). This will encourage the groups to come to early decisions about characters, relationships and situations. Stage the final tableaux together as a whole class, with the different groups, for the moment, in different areas of the room.

12. In this second stage of development, now begin 'rewinding' to show how the characters arrived at this moment. Suggest to students that they focus on these dramatic concepts. **Motivation**: having a good enough reason for the events to happen, so that the character's actions seem to 'flow' from the situation in a believable way. If a child is going to walk out of its family home for good, there has to be a good enough reason for this to happen. There has to be a logic to it.

    Back story: remember that things will have happened before these five minutes. These earlier events are part of the story of why this happens. An audience might need to understand these earlier events without actually seeing them. The past has explanatory power. How can you bring these earlier events into the scene? We might need them. It might be worth also discussing the difference between the 'living through' of these real events – as we might in a spontaneous improvisation – and constructing a performance that aims to communicate with an audience. In the second of these, we present the necessary information for the audience to understand the situation and characters and we create an experience for them.

The groups make their responses, with as much teacher involvement as you judge necessary, and with as much time offered as practical. This might be thought of as a major development in the group's approach to 'play-making'.

Drive towards performance.

A suggestion: keeping the performance within the 'drama frame', you might try going back into role as the child and watch the dramas in character through the main character's eyes. Does this capture the reality of the situation? Can they say, 'Yes, that is how it was'. This is an approach which tests the students' presentation of a plausible reality and their sense of seriousness. It offers the chance for further interrogation of the narrative.

13. After each (or all) dramas are performed, make time for discussion and responses. These will explore the narrative and the pictures they present but also the technicalities of the construction and performance of the dramas. What was seen? What did you notice? What surprised you? How was the moment made to have such impact? Which moment made you think most? Which element presented the meaning? What was the 'centre' of the piece? How might you direct the piece further?

Part Five: Back to Piccadilly: discussion

14. To bring us a sense of cyclical completeness, let's go back to the bus station. Reconstruct the pile of clothes. Explain that it's been worrying you that when you were looking at the pile of clothes *you didn't recognise the person as human.* What does this mean? Obviously, you thought it was a pile of clothes... but it wasn't. That makes you feel guilty... but it's worse than that... because even when the pile of clothes stirred and then moved... and stood... and looked at you, there was a part of you that still looked at 'it' like it was a thing... a thing to be scared of... to be embarrassed about... to shun... to turn away from. Do people sometimes treat other people like they're not human? What does that mean? I don't know.

Here, you are really testing the group's capacity to consider the meaning of the situation. You are presenting yourself as a person struggling to make sense of an event. Of course, you might feel uneasy about the moment because you are presenting the situation as one you have actually experienced. However, it seems important to the drama that this is felt as the working out of an incident that has happened in real time and real life. You might feel the need to create distance between yourself and the narrative – to preserve the veracity of your role – and frame the story, for example, as 'A man was standing at a bus stop'. If you do choose to own the narrative, it does seem an allowable deception in the honourable service of meaning-making.

15. Explain that there was an incident in the story that you didn't mention... because it wasn't very nice... and you didn't want to tell them... but you think you should. As you describe the following extension of the incident, act it out.

> *As I stood looking at the pile... someone passed you. They may have had a bit of a stagger about their walk. They had a bottle in their hand. My first thought... just from the look of them... the **scent** of them as they passed you... was that they were homeless as well... but this might not have been the case. It might just be that they were a little drunk. They looked at the pile... stopped near it... walked towards it... looked closely... looked around quickly and slyly... and then... and then began to pour the contents of their bottle over the pile of clothes smiling and laughing as they did so... and saying... 'No need for it... get off our streets... you bring shame... shame. 'And I think they would have kicked the pile... or worse... but they noticed me watching now. Took the empty bottle close to their chest, 'Waste a good...' and walked off.*
>
> *I didn't tell you because I felt (and still feel) that I should have done something... but didn't. When the child woke and stood, it was the wetness of the liquid that had woken them. When they looked at me, I think they were thinking, 'Did you see that? Did you watch that happen? Did you do nothing?'*
>
> *Here's the question: Should I feel responsible? Am I responsible for the treatment of other people? Should I have done something? What? If they had asked for money, should I have given it to them? Am I my brother's keeper?*

Discuss these questions with the group. Decide whether to take their advice.

Part Six: Around the corner

16. Where was the child going to? It was the middle of the night. It was raining. She/he had everything in a carrier bag. Had they looked at me and then decided to go home? Where they sickened by my failure to intervene? Had they looked at me and gone to a safer place...to hide? Had they had a place to go to already? Who might they have gone to meet? In *new* groups of three, invite students to discuss privately where you think she/he was going. Explain that after a few minutes you will go around each group and each group will 'try out' their idea on you. In a helpful fashion, you will be giving the groups 'permission' to continue to develop their drama; you will question and challenge their ideas in order to deepen their thinking. In a spirit of lightness, the groups will be pitching their ideas.

17. Once ideas have passed the 'audition', the groups of three will create the scene to capture just where the child goes to. To add focus and definition to the scene, indicate that whatever the scene is there will only be 15 words spoken throughout the entire sequence. Suggest that much of the rest of the time might be filled with silence. Is there any hope possible in these scenes? We don't want to find a 'happy ending', but a sense of possible future redemption might be welcome – though your students might feel this is not justified.

    Make little teacher involvement. Invite the groups to perform.

18. Discuss the work presented. Extend the discussion into a general question. Why do some of the world's richest cities have people sleeping on the streets? Is there a way forward from that situation?

19. A final moment: completing the story

    > Maybe the child was from another time or another place. Maybe I imagined him. I don't think it matters. Imagine the child gave me something. As they walked past me, they pushed something into my hand. It was a small piece of paper. It looked like this. (Produce the paper and a class set of identical papers). What could they possibly have to say to me?

    Give out the paper and invite the class to write this short final statement. This should probably be accomplished individually; a piece of slow and careful writing. Music to cover this period of reflection and expression would be helpful. Ask for the line to be written as clearly as possible so that another person can clearly read the statements.

Collect the statements together into a container...perhaps the hat that might have formed part of your pile of clothes throughout.

Standing in a circle, redistribute the statements and ask students to prepare to read the one that they now have. Suggest that the lines should be read carefully, with a moments silence between each one and with the sense that together this is one person's complete statement.

Perform the final statements.

The End.

Year 9 scheme: *Montgomery*

The Rosa Parks story is perhaps a familiar one in drama circles. I first came across it, in an early form, with Andy Jones during teacher training in Manchester. It became a staple of our work with Year 9 classes and has a unique power to capture attention and commitment. The scheme asks questions of personal responsibility and generalised citizenship: who are my responsibilities towards?

On December 1 1955 a black woman, Rosa Parks, in the city of Montgomery, Alabama, USA refused to give up her bus-seat to a white man – as was the norm on the segregated buses. This simple act marked a turning point, or rather a 'sparking point' for the American Civil Rights Movement. The resulting bus boycott brought Martin Luther King to national and international prominence for the first time.

In advance of the first phase, you will need to gather together documentary images of the period and create a power-point presentation. These are readily available online with a simple search. Our slide-show includes images of Deep South rural poverty, racist signage, segregated streets, cafés, buses, water fountains, the police, Rosa sitting on the bus and being fingerprinted, images of demonstration and boycott, MLK and finally (for later in the scheme) President Obama.

Phase 1: The bus

Part One: Setting the scene

1. Tell the story. During the telling don't mention the colour of the people involved. It is (for the moment) a story about a simple human injustice. The bus incident is to be found easily on a host of websites. We suggest that you read through several of these and having absorbed the details, develop your own storytelling narrative. Here are the bones of the story:

It is December 1 1955. The city of Montgomery, Alabama, the United States of America. A woman, 42, is waiting at a bus-stop. There are others also at the stop. The woman has been working at her job as a seamstress in a department store. When the bus arrives, she enters, pays the fare and sits about four rows back. A few stops later, the bus is full. A man enters the bus and looks for a seat at the front. There are none. He comes back to where the woman and a few others are seated and tells them to move. The others do; the woman doesn't. In a calm voice, she refuses. The passenger goes forward for the bus driver. He stops the bus and demands that she moves. She refuses. He threatens her with the police. She refuses. He calls the police. The woman thinks of her grandmother. A little later, the police arrive and arrest the woman.

2. Ask if the story is familiar. What did you not mention, that makes the story make sense? (Rosa is black.) Fill in the historical details about racial segregation in the Deep South of America in the 1950s.

Part Two: Enacting the incident

3. Whole group task. Paying due respect to the fact that this is a true story, we are going to enact the scene on the bus. Cast the scene, noting that you might re-cast later. Build the set with chairs indicating the segregated areas of the bus.
4. With you giving a more detailed narration of the scene, begin the re-enactment and pass no comment; let it run.
5. Reflect: at the end of the first run-through, ask how the group felt about it. How does it feel to be enacting this clearly 'racist' situation? Was our enactment truthful? What can we do to develop the truth of the scene?
6. Run the scene again. This time you, or members of the group, can stop the scene and comment about it if they feel it isn't 'true'. You are now the director of the scene. Freeze the scenes often. Build up a sense of social hierarchy on the bus. For example, when a new character enters the closed space of the bus, they will look down the bus and demonstrate status with eye-contact. Make the passengers a diverse group of people. Within the group, there should be some children – white or black – returning from school. Question characters. How do they feel about sitting where they are? Do they support Rosa? Where are they going on this bus? Etc. You may need to fill in details about the police. Why is it a terrifying moment when the police enter? What sort of organisation are

the police? Why would people follow laws that are patently unjust? Fear? Etc.

7. Once you have been through the whole of the scene in great detail, run it again without interruption and note the developing depth.

8. Discuss the scene. How does it feel to be in this scene? It is a racist scene? What part did you play? How did it feel to play your character?

9. We know what happened in the scene in real life. What might have happened at certain key moments? Try some *dramatic imagined events*: spontaneously create people's suggestions, running parts of the scene again and allowing these imagined events. Think particularly about what happens after Rosa is taken? Does the journey just continue? Do some leave the bus in protest?

10. Discuss with the group: Why did Rosa do this thing today? She said she wasn't particularly tired that day, nor old (as some suggested)...she was just tired of giving in. It is interesting to note that Rosa was already an 'activist' – and a member of the organisation working to end segregation.

11. Watch the slide-show of documentary images to cement the reality of life at this time. We always try to show the images as big as possible – possibly onto a large blank wall. For the moment, don't show the images of protest or the Obama slide; discuss.

Phase 2: The consequences

Part One: The cell

12. Rosa is taken and placed in a cell in the Montgomery Jailhouse. Set up the room with the chairs in a tight square. Dim the lights. This is the cell. A gap for a door. Lay down a sheet to represent the bed. In the background, play the Billy Holiday track, 'Solitude' or 'Somebody's Calling My Name' by Ry Cooder.

13. Build up a sense of the cell. Describe the graffitied walls, the filthy floor, the smell, the open toilet, the people who might normally be in the cell. Invite the group to build upon your suggestions and extend the description.

14. Discuss what Rosa might be doing here as she waits her fate. As a religious woman – she attends the Jackson Street Chapel – perhaps she prays. Place a volunteer in the space as Rosa. She is on her knees in a Christian praying position. She asks Jesus/god for help, guidance, a sign that she has done right. What is she saying to herself in her prayer? Propose that we create this prayer. Think about the tone of voice, the kinds of words she

might use in a prayer. Ask the group what she might be saying. The first person to speak will say the first line of her prayer and the speech will build line by line. Build the prayer. Once complete, repeat the lines as a continuous speech.

15. A scene: she hears people approaching and keys in the cell door. A male member of her family is about to enter. It is her husband . . . who everybody calls simply 'Parks'. You will take on this role yourself. But before doing so, ask the group to speculate on how he *might* react to her; to seeing his wife in a cell. Will he berate her for being so foolish, not thinking about the family, putting herself and him in danger? Is she too proud and stubborn? Or something else? Whatever suggestions the group make, build your characterisation about these ideas. Now enter the scene. How does Rosa react to her husband? Once the scene is enacted, you might take suggestions for how it might have gone differently . . . and try these in the style of a piece of 'forum theatre". In reality, her husband, Parks, was also a member of the NAACP who worked to end segregation and defend other black people falsely accused of crimes. Other people had done similar things to Rosa, but Rosa was chosen to be someone who would be a 'good' defendant and challenge the segregation laws in court. In a final moment, give Parks the following speech:

> *Rosa, you have done a great thing. You remember your grandmother. She remembered slavery. Though it will be difficult for you and our family; though it will bring down the wrath of the community on our heads, though our lives may be in danger and you will make us both a target for hatred and revenge . . . you have taken this first step . . . and the organising committee would like you to continue in this struggle. You could apologise now . . . pay the fine . . . walk away home . . . go back to your work as a seamstress . . . or you can stand and fight. The committee will support you. It is up to you, Rosa.*

16. Explain to the group: left alone again in her cell, Rosa must decide now: apologise and surrender, or make herself a target for hate and violence. We are now going to conduct a hot-seat in which we will explore her thinking on this important matter.

    Make this a 'distributed hot-seat' in which everyone in the group has the chance to speak as Rosa. They are still sitting as the walls of the cell – a good position to speak for her. You can question her and anybody can answer. Does she know why she did this today? Why? You are interested in why this 'ordinary' person did this extraordinary thing today. Why did this individual act on behalf of her community? Has she the strength to continue with this fight? She will be putting herself in danger. It would be easier to walk away.

17. Before she makes her final decision, the keys rattle in the door again. This time, enter as a police-officer – a kindly one. There are other people to see her. They are the children who were on the bus and witnessed her arrest. They have begged the officer to see her... perhaps pretending they were her OWN children. How old are they? Do they know her? They might usefully be a wide range of ages. The youngest is scared... but wants to know what is happening – to understand.

    Ask the group to tell you five things she might want to say to them, five things that the oldest child might be feeling, five things the youngest child might be feeling. Now, invite the group to create the scene that happens between them. There will be a Rosa and two/three children in each scene. They will perform in this space with this atmosphere.

    Key question: What do the children have to say to her? What does she have to say to them? Do they represent the wider community... and the future? What do they give her?

    Prepare. Watch.

18. After watching these scenes, reflect upon what decision she might take. How has their visit influenced her? Does it give her a sense of greater social responsibility? Does she feel her actions can transform their world?

Part Two: The jailhouse steps: a scripted scene

In this phase, we shift mode to explore the next scene through a whole-group scripted piece. On occasions, a large class has been divided into two and rehearsed two versions of the same scene. However, there is much to be said for working the whole class as a large cast and directing the scene yourself as you might for a production. This gives an insight into production processes.

The scene is actually from a large-scale musical play that was written for our Manchester school about the history of protest and social progress. It was called Promised Land.

19. Explain:

> Rosa's protest becomes very well-known very quickly. People are both inspired by and angry at her. At the bottom of the steps of the jailhouse

where she is being held two crowds have gathered. She can hear them through her cell window. One is a crowd who are against her and one is a crowd who have come to support her. Leading this crowd is the new young preacher of Rosa's chapel, Rev. Martin Luther King.

Tell the group: we are going to work on a fictitious version of this scene using the script. We don't know that this scene even happened…but it might have done…and it might have been like this. We are going to stage the scene as we might if we were a theatre company putting on the play.

20. Read the scene. Cast it. Block it. Direct it. Work it. Perform it. Your preparations might include the making of the placards mentioned or research on accents.

At the foot of the Montgomery Jailhouse steps.
Music.
An armed police officer stands guard at the top of the steps.
In a flat area – a public square at the bottom of the steps – are a group of calm protestors. They are walking around slowly in a circle with placards reading: 'End Segregation', 'We will not ride on segregated buses', 'We'd rather walk', 'Free Rosa Parks' etc. They may be humming a hymn, perhaps, 'Swing Low Sweet Chariot' or similar. Martin is amongst them. At the other end of the stage are an angry group. They are shouting at the protestors.

Phoenix   She's lucky we let her on our bus in the first place.
Cooper   Segregation is a way of life; the South's way.
Hampton   I hear Rosa's husband is too weak to keep her down. He's gonna whip her himself.

Parks, Rosa's husband is one of the protestors. He starts to move out of the circle. Martin stops him.

Martin   Now, that's exactly what they want. You're given 'em rope to hang ya. We gotta remain calm. Justice is on our side.

Inside the jailhouse. James F. Blake, the bus driver, is preparing to leave.

Officer   Now, we can sneak you out the back if you prefer, Mr Blake. It's gettin' pretty ugly outside.

Driver   I ain't gonna sneak away like I done something wrong. I gotta face 'em. It were my bus.

Outside. One of the angry crowd throws something at the protestors. No reaction.

Hampton (Shouting) Hell, this is gonna be like shooting cans off a fence. These cowards don't fight back.
Pike   (Shouting) I seen old Sheriff Bull on TV saying he ain't never gonna allow blacks to sit at the front of the buses.
Martin   (Loud so they can hear) The truth don't need to shout. Justice sings a silent song.

The driver appears at the top of the steps. The crowd react noisily.

Cox   Here comes our boy.

The angry crowd are cheering. The driver straightens himself and begins to walk down the steps. The protestors part quietly to allow him passed. When he is in the middle of the space between the two crowds, Martin steps forward.

Martin   Sir. Can I ask you? Are you happy with what you done?

The driver stops.

Colwyn   Don't you listen to that Communist.

The angry crowd cheer. The driver turns to them.

Driver   Won't you people stop hollering. Ya sound like a pack of farm animals.

They are quiet. He turns to Martin.

Driver   Mister, I'm just the guy who drives the bus.
Martin   A segregated bus.
Driver   I don't make the rules, friend, I just bin taught to obey them.
Martin   Those laws deprive us of our humanity.

Driver	**(Waits)** I know that sir. **(Quiet)**
Martin	This is a time of change.
Driver	**(Looks up)** It surely is.
Parks	We ain't gonna ride your buses no more. **(The protestors agree.)**
Driver	I aint no foolish red-neck. Rules are rules. I see the whole world steppin' on and off my bus. Seems to me we all appreciate a little respect. Perhaps we even all deserve it. **(Wait)** I gotta follow the rules. I don't know no other way. Till the rules are changed. **(Looking at the angry crowd)** Something's rotten when people go whippin' up an anger. Anger makes fools of all of us. **(Wait)** I gotta go.

The angry crowd parts quietly for him.

The End.

Part Three: The bus driver

21. Discuss with the group: does anything surprise you about the scene? How does the bus driver come across? What is his attitude? How does he respond to the angry crowd? What sort of person do you think he is? What is his family life like? Being a driver for the city is a good job – he wears a smart uniform and hat. He served his country in the second world war. He is a law-abiding citizen. Is he a 'good man'? What might his home life be like? Is he a good father, a good husband?

22. Propose that the class tries to imagine the driver's home life on that day. Students are going to produce a flashback to the driver's arrival at home *before* the events of the scripted scene. In the time-line of his day, it is after he has finished work and Rosa has been arrested, but before he has been called to the police station to make a statement. As the driver, he himself was required to sign the warrant for her arrest. He is arriving home. At home there is just his wife and one or two children.

23. To help develop the scene, propose the following details and questions:
    ● As he enters from work it is clear there is something wrong: a long silence.
    ● Is the child/children asked to leave the room? Do they? Do they overhear and return?
    ● His wife already knows what has happened. Has it been on the news? Has someone called her with the news? How does she feel about her

husband's job and the segregation laws? Is it something they have discussed before?

● How does he feel about the laws he upholds? What will he say when he makes his statement? His job . . . a very good job . . . could be on the line.

● He knows that crowds are gathering at the jailhouse. There will be violence. He must attend to make a statement. Are his responsibilities to his family, his job or to his 'society'? Is it possible that he spends his life enforcing rules that he does not agree with? (Or is this our fantasy?)

● We know his attitude at the steps. What does he wish to say in his statement? Will he dare to defend Rosa's action? What would this mean for him and his family? How does he arrive at the decision to go there and what is his intention when he gets there?

● How will he explain what has happened today to his child? How will he explain the segregation laws that are all around them? Does the child need them explaining?

Groups now create this scene. They will be performed and reflected upon.

Part Four: The cell and Rosa's dream

24. Following the performance of these scenes, shift the focus back to Rosa in the cell. Narrate:

It is later. Rosa is alone. She has heard the shouting and aggression from the square below . . . and knows that she has caused it. The street is quiet now. As the police officer, enter the cell. You are scared. You say the whole city is going to go up in flames; this was the spark that some had been waiting for. The streets will run with blood – and the black community will be the victims. Does Rosa want this on her conscience? Can't she see this is just the South's way . . . it'll never change. You offer her a final chance to 'recant', to apologise, to go home and keep her head down. He leaves a piece of paper – an apology he has written for her to sign – along with a pen and exits. Should she give in? Is the violence and bloodshed that will come worth the cost? Should she carry on the fight? Should she return to a quiet life? Is she prepared to die? What would you do? Discuss.

25. Rosa is asleep. In her sleep she is visited by two people who do not exist; one because he is already dead and one because he is not yet born. Who might they be and what do they want to say to her that will help her make her decision? The past and the future speak to her; it is a vision and one in which you might yourself have a dialogue with Rosa. This is to be our final piece of drama on this subject. We will need to consider how to act, move and speak like a person who does not exist; how to preserve a sense of 'otherness' and to build a non-naturalistic drama. You are going to create this scene as a final statement. Who will you put into Rosa's dream?

26. Create. Prepare. Rehearse. Direct. Perform.

Final thoughts

27. Give some details of the events that follow from this night. We know that Rosa continued in her struggle and this was a key moment in the Civil Rights Movement. Tell of Martin Luther King and the Montgomery bus boycott: black people refused to ride the segregated buses. It took months, even years ... but the laws were changed. Martin Luther King became a spokesman for the movement – we all know his famous speech in Washington – He was murdered in Memphis in 1968. Discuss the processes of history. Consider the truth in this statement: 'The world tends towards greater justice'. Is the world more just than in was in the past? How do things change? What is the role of individuals in this change? Should we be concerned about making the world a fairer place?

  Look at the power-point again. This time include all of the scenes of protest, the march on Washington and King's speech, Rosa as an old woman, the bus in the museum as a piece of history and a final slide of President Obama, perhaps with his aspirational slogan, 'Yes, we can'.

The End.

Year 9 scheme: *Detention*

In this scheme of work students are invited to explore the character of a young criminal. The scheme quickly becomes an exploration of what might be termed a totalitarian system, with the teacher taking on a substantial role as the governor of the prison. This is a demanding, high-status role for you but also a very important one in terms of taking a full part in the narrative and demonstrating technique and commitment.

From a drama point of view this is our first sortie into full character development.

It is also a scheme which explores the processes of the criminal justice system and allows the group to consider society's and their own attitudes to crime and punishment; the criminal and the punished.

You will need to prepare some information about the criminal justice system in your own area. Where would people of your students' ages be incarcerated? What would such a place be called? Are there different levels or varieties of institution? Whatever such places might be called ... your governor, in a no-nonsense fashion, will simply call it a 'prison' ... and so shall we.

This is a scheme of work that has its origins right back with Dorothy Heathcote and her 'Prisoner X' narrative. This is as recounted by Mark Wheeler in his *Drama Schemes* book. It came to me originally, again, through my teacher training in Manchester. My own recount here, is as it has developed and evolved over some 18 years of classroom practie. I dedicate it to Dorothy and you – who might take it into the future.

Phase 1: Preparation for role

Part One: Opening discussion

1. At different times in our history different groups of people have been 'criminalised' or 'scape-goated'. That is, a specific group of people are singled out to be blamed for society's problems and treated with suspicion.

These people are treated as criminals just because of who they are and the group they belong to. A particular feature of their group is that they are viewed as 'outsiders' to the mainstream society. What groups might these be? Discuss this honestly and widely. In our experience, we arrive quite quickly at a consideration of young people as such a group.

Part Two: Story-telling

2. Ask for brief stories where the students may have been treated with suspicion by somebody because they are young. Students tell stories. (For example being followed in a shop, being met with aggression, fear). Why do people have this idea about young people? Has it always been like this? Do young people deserve the suspicion, the fear? Are you and your friends a gang? Are you seen as one?

Part Three: Drama set-up

3. If it is true that the label of criminality is sometimes placed upon you, in this drama you are going to accept the label – for the purposes of drama – and say, 'OK, we are'. The drama that is about to begin puts you all in a young offender's institute. You are all individuals with a very particular story to tell. You have all been arrested, questioned, tried, convicted and sentenced. You all have different attitudes towards your crime and your incarceration. Your families all have different reactions to your crime as well. Your first task will be to begin to build a character; a 'person' distinct from yourself who is rooted in reality and who you think you could play convincingly. You might have an image in your head of someone you have met or seen or even know. You might have a fact, or a name. Whatever your starting point, you are going to 'build out' from this simple reality to create a character.

4. Discuss the characters with a partner. Each person needs to decide how old they are, what crime they are in 'prison' for and how their families feel about them being 'inside'. Each person must prepare:

    ● a solo tableau of the moment you committed the crime. What thought was going through your head when it happened? Prepare this line alongside the tableau (eg: 'It's only a TV'). At this point each person may wish to think about the 'kind' of crime that might be committed by these young people. This will not be a high security prison. Warn the group: the decisions you take now you must live with until the end of the scheme; choose your crime and your attitude carefully, this will be the root of the person you are going to create, your character.

- your family's attitude towards your crime. What did your closest relative (e.g. mother, father, etc) say when the police told them that you had been arrested? Invent the line that he/she spoke. Were they shocked, angry, amused, distraught, embarrassed, guilty, ashamed? Something else? Invent the line and give it to your partner to say.

5. Pair performance: a pair at a time perform their tableau and lines. Each person drops into the tableau. They then speak the line that accompanies and clarifies their crime. After a pause their partner performs their family's reaction line. We witness the variety of crimes and the variety of reactions, attitudes and feelings.

By the end of the first phase you have achieved two things; engaged the students' own experience with the situation that is about to enfold and rooted the creation of character in action and community. There is a juvenile excitement sometimes (particularly with some boys) in the creation of a 'criminal' character. By performing the character's thought and the family's reaction, both expressed with an emotion charge, we attempt to touch a deeper level of commitment to the reality of the role.

Phase 2: Into role

Part One: Creating the prison environment

6. Discuss the prison:
   - **As a physical space:** Either in advance, or now as a group, draw a simple map or representation of the building. What would you expect to find: cells, canteen, offices, work rooms, classroom, etc. Such locations help to both build the reality of the world and suggest locations for later action.
   - **As an institutional space:** It is a place with a strict regime. The governor believes that it needs to be a tough place to deter the young from re-offending. S/he is a powerful character, ruling with a 'rod of iron'. What sort of restrictions or behaviours might this mean for the lives of our prisoners? What is a typical day like? How might they speak about the prison regime? Of course, they might think that the governor is right to be tough on them.
7. Set-up the scene:
   - Explain that it is Thursday morning, 'session time'. The governor has been instructed by prison authorities within the government to listen to

inmates' problems/suggestions on a regular basis. *This* governor thinks it's a ridiculous waste of time but does it anyway. In a few moments you (the teacher) are going to go outside and come back in 'in role'. There are two things that are important when you re-enter:

i.   That the inmates must sit in a perfect circle (the governor like things perfect).

ii. When you enter they must stand very straight in silence and wait to be asked to sit and speak. The governor will not tolerate anything other than obedience.

Part Two: Taking up roles

8. Enter as the governor. You exude power! You enjoy your authority. You are dangerous. You take no nonsense! You demonstrate high-status body language. If individuals do take you on, we must assume that they are new! You must win. Take away privileges, threaten worse, make them reveal their crime. Let them know that you have total control of their lives. You decide when they eat, sleep, walk about, etc. If the group do not submit to your authority you may need to good-naturedly and temporarily step out of role and explain the group's responsibility for helping to establish your character as a high-status figure with real authority over their lives. We have to settle into the lives lived in this place and behave within the conditions of this situation; we have to accept the 'given circumstances'. In this situation their characters know you and the context thoroughly. (Though we might also celebrate the group's tendency to kick against such a controlling presence.)

9. Around the circle ask students to stand and admit their crime. They have prepared for this in Phase 1. Claim full knowledge of their lives . . . you have their records in your office. You know about their families, their schools, their previous scrapes with the law. Pillory them. You are on the side of 'decent', 'law-abiding citizens', you regard criminals as 'scum'.

10. Develop the context: this 'meeting/session' time is a weekly forum for inmates to make their complaints and observations about life in the institute. Following character introductions ask for the inmates' complaints about life in the prison (food, TV, etc). You are impatient with their 'whingeing'. You don't give a damn! Ridicule every complaint. Come prepared with your own set of complaints from inmates which they have anonymously put in a 'suggestion box'. This allows you to introduce your own ideas and to draw a fuller picture of life here, e.g. work schedule, visiting times, etc.)

11. Turn the tables. It is time for *your* complaints. Develop a sense of danger. A crime has been committed: during work detail yesterday two items were stolen from a member of staff, a packet of cigarettes and a five pound note. Anyone know anything? No. You are about to conduct a search of the whole wing. You believe the items are still here somewhere. Dismiss the group with instructions for them to return to their cells immediately.

12. Out of role, discuss briefly the group's responses to the governor and their characters' situation. Is the regime justified? Fair? How do they reflect upon the character of the governor? What is his/her motivation? How does it feel to be under such an authority's control?

13. Now move on to explain that to develop understanding of their characters, students must:

    ● Decide who they share their cells with. One or two others. How do they get on together? In choosing cell-mates it is very useful to think about making the characters in each cell different from each other. Usual friendship groups won't be the most productive groups; they arrived here as strangers and the governor will have determined who gets to share.

    ● Use the available furniture to build their cells. You (or the groups) might mark out the limited size of the different cells with masking tape on the floor. This could include doors, windows, beds etc. A simple task which again adds a new layer of reality.

    ● Create a scene between the people in your cell. The governor doesn't search immediately. S/he makes you wait. What are they doing whilst they wait? How do they feel about being here? What are they saying about their family? These simple scenes should reveal more about each character and establish the relationships between them.

    ● Decide what objects the inmates might have that they do not want the governor to find? These could be simple things: letters, photographs or banned items such as mobile phones. These objects might be simply created out of paper and masking tape.

    Note: No one has to have the stolen items. *You* will decide who has them. Students rehearse their scenes.

14. Using the settings created around the room, perform all of the scenes of preparation. This demonstrates character, relationships and gives you information which you can use in the scenes that follow.

15. As the governor, conduct the search immediately after the last group has performed. You need to decide in advance which group has the cigarettes and money. This must be a group that includes students who will be able

to handle a demanding set of roles later on. It is best if the group has three in it. As you conduct the search continue to underline and perhaps abuse your authority. Turn over their furniture, find the objects made of paper, rip down photographs, find personal letters and rip them, steal valuable items, use information you have just gained from their scenes. Go to the chosen group last. At the end of the final scene find the stolen items. Question them briefly. Send them outside the room.

16. Word goes around the wing that someone has been caught and what has happened to them. What rumours? Whisper these rumours from cell to cell. Perhaps the story changes, develops, magnifies as it is told repeatedly. The situation has suddenly become desperate. There seems to be no way out of the present situation for the inmates. Crystallise the sense of hopelessness with a quick 'sentence root' exercise: 'This prison, a place of...'.

The night-time cell

17. You need a little time now to prime the group you have chosen for the next section. In this short piece of small-group play-making you attempt again to allow students the chance to face the realities of their characters' situation. Explain that they spend a long time in their cell with these other people. Three major sources of a sense of depression for them are lack of privacy, boredom and lack of contact with their families. At night the feelings become more acute. It is past midnight. You are all in your bunks. The atmosphere is subdued and heavy. Instruct the group to prepare this scene.

18. In the meantime you speak to the three students who had been in the offending cell:
    - One of the prisoners is never seen again. The governor says that he/she has been 'transferred for their own safety'. This actor comes back in as the inspector of prisons, Lord X. This is the governor's boss, conducting a spot check of the prison.
    - Another prisoner comes back in with terrible injuries. S/he says s/he has 'fallen down the stairs'.
    - The third prisoner comes back and is now governor's 'favourite'. Terrified and giving all the right answers.

19. Night-time scene performances. Students perform the scenes. A subdued, reflective atmosphere.

Session time

20. Ask students to return to their circle for weekly session. Ask them to be in role and waiting for you. Tell them that it is now three weeks after the theft.
21. Session time begins. In role explain what has happened since the theft. You are edgy. You bring in the absent prisoners one at a time and explain what has happened to them both. The first carries his/her injuries, the other is now warmly welcomed by you in a strained new relationship of friendship; the group are left to read the implications of both entrances. You explain, with a sense of threat, that the third 'offender' has been moved to another establishment. You are lying on all counts. Now explain that a government inspector has turned up (much to your irritation). Explain your feelings about the liberal establishment/the Home Office. The inspector will take part in today's session. Threaten them all to behave and to not mention the theft. 'Lord X is going back to his castle at 4 o'clock, *I* shall be staying here.'

    Bring in the inspector. You are sycophantic. Be suddenly nice and respectful to prisoners. Tell inmates that the session will continue 'as normal'. Listen to their complaints with sympathy. Promise to do things. The effect is likely to be comic, but stay fully in role. Rely upon your 'new favourite' prisoner and the injured one to give the right answers at awkward moments.

    It is almost guaranteed that someone will dare to challenge your audacious hypocrisy, or indeed to mention the theft and the 'disappeared' inmate. If it doesn't happen naturally then centre upon the injured prisoner and provoke dissent with your pressure. A crunch moment! Will this prisoner tell the inspector what really happened to him/her or continue to stay under the authority of the governor? The pressure will come from both sides: you and the group.

    During this session you may need to prompt the inspector to question you by whispering in his/her ear out of role. Suggest that the inspector asks you to leave so that you can talk to prisoners alone.

    The inspector asks you to leave. You refuse. You are worried. The inspector insists. You threaten the inmates with a dangerous smile, perhaps indicating the CCTV cameras high in the corners of the room. You warn the inspector regarding the nature of the inmates: s/he shouldn't trust them. Your façade is slipping. You leave. The session continues without you. The 'favourite' prisoner may continue to defend you. The injured prisoner may not yet have told the truth. They can do so now. The group takes authority and knows that it needs these two characters to tell the truth. Will they buckle under the weight of their peers? It is important to the whole community that the truth is told. This becomes a dramatic imperative. We are absorbed now in a moment of spontaneous improvisation.

At this point you can re-enter out of role and watch. You may need to explain that you are no longer in role. If necessary you can intervene in the action, make suggestions, give it shape, perhaps whispering privately to some characters at certain moments as necessary.

Finally you (in role as the governor) are brought back in. The inspector says what s/he is going to do. This will probably involve making further investigations; suspending but not removing you immediately. You explode at the inspector. You express your beliefs about making prison a deterrent. You attack 'woolly-minded, liberal do-gooders' etc. The inspector leaves with you. The prisoners probably want to rejoice and jeer the governor off the wing. Stop.

Part Three: Cliff-hanger

22. Ask students what they think will happen next. Discuss the realities of the situation. Could this happen? Do we live in a society where our basic human rights are protected by the law? A governor behaving like this would, we expect, be dealt with. But watch the following . . .

23. Explain to the group who has ultimate responsibility for prisons. This will be an elected politician: in Britain, the Home Secretary. Tell them that X is the Home Secretary. As the inspector exits the governor goes straight to his office. He sits down in his plush leather chair and makes a phone call. He is calling the Home Secretary's private mobile number. Act out the telephone conversation that the governor now has. The Home Secretary is a very old friend of the governor. The governor chats with him about their children. He laughs, friendly and sycophantic. Then, the governor complains about the inspector. They seem to agree about him being 'soft'. He asks the Home Secretary to intervene. He is calling in a favour. The Home Secretary 'owes' the governor. Is it a blackmail situation? The Home Secretary promises to make sure the inspector's report is silenced. As a final flourish, the governor reminds the Home Secretary of his/her promise to provide funding for more CCTV cameras. The governor puts the phone down. His power is secure. He smiles.

This can be a very powerful section of drama in which students are able to experience the sense of entrapment in an inescapable social situation. It is time to discuss these things and to pinpoint historical and cultural examples of the totalitarian state. The governor tries to exercise control over all aspects of the inmates' lives, to control information, to rewrite stories, to use threat and, potentially, violence itself.

At the same time you have demonstrated the techniques of high-status characterisation: how to communicate power. In the last phase you have also demonstrated the dramatic power of nuance and a kind of dramatic irony; how to lie to the inspector in a situation where all observers understand the lie but are suppressed in their response.

It is always impressive how the group of inmates will finally take on the authority of the governor. The final clincher, however, is an equally impressive retort to the growing sense of community action.

Phase 3: Reflections

Part One: Focus on theme

24. Talk about crime and punishment. In this drama everyone seems to have accepted that prisoners should be treated with respect. But doesn't the governor have a point about punishment and deterrence? How should a prisoner be treated? Does someone who has broken the law have rights? Some would say they have given up their right to be treated well. Is this right? How would their victims want them treated? Are the victims the best people to decide on punishment? Don't be surprised if students are signif-icantly 'right wing' in their sentiments regarding criminals. Now ask:

    Why, when you acted the characters of the inmates, did you not give the same answers? You seem to say in your answers now that prison should be a deterrent, it should be tough. Now you seem to agree with the governor! Could this be true…? When you answered with 'imagination' (through the character) you instinctively treated your characters with respect and sympathy; we might say 'with more humanity'. I wonder which set of beliefs is the one which is your 'real' answer?

Part Two: Focus on drama skills

25. Whilst we've been acting we've not really thought about drama skills…we've just been using them. Now let's think about them:
    - **The governor** How did I act the governor? In particular, how did I show that s/he was powerful? Introduce the term 'high status body language'.

What is this? You may need to drop back into character for the demonstration. Get students to notice the details of your body language. Posture, eye contact, pace of movement and speech, stillness. Demonstrate the opposite. It doesn't work. Ask students to volunteer to be the governor. It is the start of 'Session'. The governor enters. Try it several times. After each attempt ask the class to 'read' the body language.

- **Character building** At the very start you were asked to invent three things about your character. These are all things that are not true about you (apart from your age perhaps). The job of an actor is to create 'another person', to invent their story, their feelings, their situations. You have been asked since then to make sure that your character is different from other characters. Characters are unique just like people...you are not just a 'criminal'. Now we're going to concentrate for a time on your character.

Part Three: Visiting time

26. You were asked how your family felt about you being in prison. We are now going to use this information. We are going back into prison. It is one month later. The governor is still in charge. It is visiting time. The governor is patrolling. The situation is described like this:

- There is a strong feeling of defeat amongst the prisoners.
- Each inmate is going to be visited by their closest relative. (Or the one who *will* visit them). You must prepare a scene between the two of you. It must be clear how they and you feel.
- Rules say that any items passed to prisoners must be passed to the governor first for inspection.
- In the scene you should receive news from home. Your visitor may have brought you something.
- In the scene you may want to tell them about the governor and the situation in the prison. The inspector seems to have done nothing. You have lost faith. You believe the gossip that says that the missing prisoner is dead. The CCTV cameras are now an immense element of the situation.

Note: You may decide to make two versions of the same scene with students swapping roles so that each gets to play their prisoner, or you may make the creation of the relative the focus of a new acting job. This encourages complexity.

Now make the scene.

Performance

27. There will be two performances of this scene. Firstly, set the room as a visiting room in the prison. TIR as the governor. Visitors and prisoners wait outside the 'room'. Talk them into role . . . how do they feel? What are they expecting? Bring the two groups in one at a time. As the prisoners enter, suggest that they act the impact of the CCTV cameras on their behaviour and attitude and let the scenes run in real time and concurrently, without an audience. The governor patrols. Secondly, at the end of this 'real time' run, send students to the edges of the room, clearing the 'set' and invite each pair to perform their scene again on their own.

Reflect

28. How does it feel to be performing these characters? Do you still feel as sympathetic towards them? When you watch others act their characters how do you know that they're 'in character'? The governor has maintained control of the prison and your life. Has anybody, during visiting, managed to get information out to the world about conditions in the 'prison'? Perhaps they have, in which case use this situation. If they haven't, narrate a situation in which an inmate managed to pass a long and desperate letter to a family member. This prepares us for the final section.

Phase 4: Assessment

In this final phase, we make available our character set, the situation and the setting for a piece of summative self-directed drama. The change of form allows the group to process and present their lived-through experience in a new way – to transfer their understanding and imagined worlds across perspectives. They now need to think more analytically through the eyes of an observer.

You might find it useful to make this final small-group play-making task an assessed pieced – one for which all of the preceding work might be considered a study.

The proposal involves the creation of a 'documentary'. Ordinarily, this would be a televisual format. You might feel able to make this a filmed drama, should resources and time allow, but it is also possible to take the documentary format and give it a staged reading. Indeed, in Britain recently, there has been a fashion for making a kind of 'documentary theatre' which takes real events, reports and spoken words and creates a dramatic, staged piece as a form of campaigning tool. You might consider using this idea and accounting for it from within the context of the drama.

29. Where could this story possibly end? Are the prisoners doomed and helpless? The truth has not left the prison. Has an authority like the governor really got such freedom to do as they wish? Even the most powerful institutions can be 'blown open' by the media (in Britain, think about the parliamentary expenses scandal, or the BBC/Saville scandal).

Part One: Trial by television (or theatre)

30. Are our press/media/theatres relatively free to criticise authority? In the final phase of this scheme we are going to create drama-documentaries in which the governor and prison is put 'on trial'. It will be an 'exposé' of this prison. (Though leave open the possibility of a documentary which supports the governor against the slander of the inmates.) Groups will use the characters, situations, events of our drama to construct a drama (again, as filmed, acted-TV documentary or theatre-piece) to tell the world about life in the prison. It is part of a campaign to end the governor's regime.

31. Discuss the documentary form. A documentary might include: interviews with main characters (these might be combatative), interviews with 'experts', voice-overs, reconstructions of events, secret camera work, CCTV footage, etc.

If electing for the 'filmed' version it might be wise to ask for a simple two minute news report. Remember you will need to leave time for editing.

The groups will probably need to be quite large. All of the chief roles in the narrative so far should be taken by students.

It might be helpful to make large pieces of paper available for planning. A key early question might be: which elements of our work should be brought in here to paint a picture of prison life? How can this be shown?

Explain that this extended task will be assessed and what your criteria will be.

Groups prepare.

Groups perform.

Part Two: The governor

32. Finally, seal the drama with a return to the governor. Is he finally brought down? Perhaps by the intervention of the media? Or does he survive but have moments of regret, dread, doubt or fear? Late at night, in the privacy of his own mind, does he suffer for what he has done?

33. In the form of a distributed hot-seat, send the whole group to their own
    isolated space. All are to be the governor; now revealed as a fearful broken
    man. You are to interview him. Anyone can answer your questions. Take it
    slowly. Leave him powerless.

*In this final moment, we don't simply want to rehabilitate the character of the
governor, we want to give students a sense of authority over him; to offer an
image and an experience of the fallen mighty.*

The End.

Year 9/10 scheme: *Hamlet*

Not only are the works of Shakespeare iconic and central to our dramatic culture, they also represent rich seams of human experience which, if we can gain access to them for our young people, offer possibilities for exploring important questions and aspects of life in exactly the ways that have been described throughout this book. When we inhabit Shakespeare's great stories we place our work and ourselves at those human extremities where meaning is made; whether tragic or otherwise. Of all the famous characters, images and language of the Shakespearean canon, Hamlet perhaps offers us the most iconic. Through an accessible exploration, young people can gain authority over the narrative, the character, the language – the icons themselves. We come to a new relationship with the lives lived and they *speak to us* is profound ways. The play isn't great because it stems from our cultural giant, but because it has such use to us here and now. On the shoulders of the giant we see further than we ever could alone.

Hamlet is a play which very much centres upon Hamlet himself; his situation and how he struggles to cope with it. In this presentation of the character, he is a young man captured in a circumstance not of his making, but required to 'right' it. 'O cursèd spite! That ever I was born to set it right.' He has a direct relationship with the audience and speaks to them frequently. They share in his intimate explorations of the meaning of his situation and his responses to it; he is an elemental meaning-maker: 'To be or not to be, that is the question'. In drama-in-education terms, Hamlet is a compulsive 'thought-tracker'. Aside from the soliloquising and elaborate (and wonderful) reflections on life, the play is also a swashbuckling story of families, murder, revenge, plots, ghosts and comeuppance.

The scheme approaches the text through the eyes of the population of the village at the foot of the royal home, Elsinore Castle. This pre-text phase inducts students into the world of the play; the characters they create are a bridge into the castle; they are the 'self-creations' that we use as vehicles to encounter Shakespeare's people.

Phase 1: Into Hamlet's world

Part One: Five funerals at Elsinore

1. Prepare the drama space: darken the room and throw a projected image of the castle in a dominant position. Light some candles. Using simple piles of material/sheeting build a centre-piece arrangement which suggests five bodies lying in state in the crypt of the castle. This is easier than it might sound. The key element is to make the underlying shapes as humanoid as possible – the head and feet being important indicators – and then lay flat sheeting over the body-reliefs so that the construction is hidden and the image is 'good enough' to spike the imagination into belief. The darkness and candle light is particularly significant here. Each shape will have a prop item to indicate character: a crown, a book, a cup, a sword and a flower.

2. Meet the group outside the space. Explain that as soon as they enter the drama will have begun. Give a few details of the narrative and setting.

   Explain that you will be acting as a particular person and so will they. They are all peasant villagers who live near the castle and are going to be let in secretly, to see terrible sights – to see their royal family, to visit the crypt. Having established the atmosphere and built expectation in a playful way, lead the group to the door of the prepared drama space. You will be the gravedigger. The gravedigger is an auxiliary character in the play. Hamlet stumbles upon him as he digs Ophelia's grave – an exchange that gives rise to the 'Alas, poor Yorick' reflection. We use him here as a guide into the world of the play.

   We offer a suggested text for the gravedigger below, but you will, of course, improvise around this.

   We begin right in the heart of the world of the play: a whole-group drama driven by a teacher-in-role (TIR) character. The TIR is a compelling way of bringing the group into the drama and an efficient way of giving over essential information in a compelling format.

   Explain:

   Most of you have never been in the castle, this is an important day for you. You might live in its shadow, see it every day, but for most of you this is the first time you've been inside. You are being allowed in because anarchy has broken out… the Royal House of Denmark is in turmoil. You are only being brought in as an act of subversion by the irreverent gravedigger. This is the crypt… where bodies are kept. When we enter, breathe in the atmosphere: the sounds, feeling, look, of the crypt. When you enter, I want you to tell me what you see and how you feel. Now enter.

3.   The gravedigger is a no-nonsense, earthy labourer. He has no respect for the royals that now lie at his feet...we are all worm-meat waiting for the work of his spade. He has sympathy for some of them but his irreverence shows his distrust of authority and his proto-democratic aspirations. Finding his voice might be important.

Part Two: The gravedigger speaks

4.   As they enter the room, greet them immediately as the gravedigger. You have the tools of your trade – spade and rope – about you and lead them into the darkened room with a candle lantern.

> *Arrr...ya come did ya? Thought you didn't believe me last night in the inn. Well, glad you did. I got such things to show ya. Things as you won't believe. Come wi' me now. But think on...You shouldn't be here. This is a dangerous place tonight. There's an army come...and it's said that spirits walk the halls and passages...and from what I can see...with kings and queens and princes lying dead...there ain't no-one in charge. That won't last. So before the castle is made a closed fortress...I'll take you in. It's good for the ruled to see their rulers laid low...does ya good, I think. Come...*

He leads them towards the crypt.
As he opens the door he bangs his shovel on the floor.

> *Gotta scare off the rats afore we go in.*

He leads them in and stands the group in a circle around the arrangement of corpses.

> *Behold! Your royal family! How the mighty have fallen! Don't they look small...you'd think they were children lyin' under these sheets. But I tell you...I saw them fall. I carried their weight and lay them here...I gathered their things and placed them beside them.*
>   *But for the Lady Ophelia here, they died within just five minutes of each other. In the Great Hall that lies right above us here. Their royal*

blood ran through the cracks and dripped to where they now lie. Listen.

(He evokes the sound of the drip and other sounds of the environment of the crypt . . . perhaps inviting the group to join in with the sounds to create an impromptu soundscape: the scurry of rats; the howl of the wind; the distant rolling of the icy sea.)
He introduces the characters.

Behold. The king, Claudius. The bringer of sorrow. Brother to the good old king. Some say despot . . . some say, viper . . . some say murderer. Here lies the crown of the House of Denmark. Three kings in three months . . . dead . . . is this crown cursed? Three kings in three months . . . the old king Hamlet died in the orchard in mysterious circumstances . . . some say poisoned by an asp, a snake. Then this king . . . old Hamlet's brother. Died with a dagger to the heart, not one full day ago. And on the self same day . . . he who would have been king next . . . young Hamlet . . . run through with a poison rapier. Young blood spilt on the floor above. I'll bury that crown . . . None shall wear it . . . it'll lie with the wasted House of Denmark.

See here . . . by Hamlet's side. The last book he read . . . will go unfinished now. I'll bury it with him . . . no eyes shall see it.

And see here . . . a mother's shame . . . to lie cold beside her only child . . . Her son Hamlet . . . whose heart she broke with the too-hasty marrying of his uncle. This, the cup that was at her lips at the moment she fell. One sip . . . and the queen be gone.

And here . . . she who would have been our queen . . . the Lady Ophelia . . . Lady to the young Hamlet . . . taken beneath the glassy waters in the days before yesterday's bloody end. Her brother and her Hamlet fought within her grave . . . one freshly dug by these hands . . . in unconsecrated ground. She showed me kindness once . . . and I would not have her lie in such a grave. Here the flower she reached for . . . the last flower she picked. Before the branch snap and she fall into the waiting water. O, what a tragedy this . . .

And her brother . . . the gentleman Laertes . . . embittered by the loss of father and sister . . . at Hamlet's foolish hand. Destined to die in the royal hall of blood.

Behold, my villagers all . . . Your mighty, mighty royals . . . whose time to fall has come.

5. At the end of your introductory speech, step out of role and ask the group what they have just gleaned from the Gravedigger. Demonstrate the key starting relationships *in space* with four students playing the four roles of the Old King, Claudius, Gertrude and Hamlet. Make a simple *statue of relationships* to cement understanding with you simply narrating.

Part Three: The villagers talk

6. Now, return to the drama. The gravedigger hears something in the passage outside. He doesn't want to get caught. It is said that young Fortinbras is to take over…and he isn't yet to be trusted; he may be as vicious as Claudius. The gravedigger leaves the room to investigate, telling the villagers to be quiet. You can then return out of role and ask the group to continue in role and to discuss as a group their reactions to the gravedigger's account. Is he to be believed? How do they feel about the king now? About Hamlet? What gossip have they heard that will add or support the account given? How do they feel about the royal corpses lying before them now?

7. Invite the group to take up a tableau one at a time to show their attitude towards this royal household or a member of it. You might extend the moment by asking students to individually come forward and speak their thoughts on the marriage and the deaths: 'It's not right, the old king's body's still warm!' or 'That king was cruel, I'm glad he's dead. I spit on his body…'

8. Coming out of role, discuss this now complete moment of induction into the narrative and characters. We know that the story will end in bloodshed. Is this a story that seems worth pursuing? Of course it does. Explain that in the following sections we will explore a range of moments, situations, themes of the play.

Phase 2: Hamlet and the wedding

Part One: Becoming Hamlet

9. Explain that we have just visited the end of the story, but that Shakespeare's play begins soon after the wedding of Claudius and Gertrude. How does Hamlet walk around the castle at this time? How is he feeling? How does his body show this? Give names to how he feels.

    Quickly invite everyone to form a pair and then agree who will be 'A's and who 'B's. (this is for a slightly later task). Now invite everyone to find a space on their own and to respond to the following:

You are Hamlet. There is a wedding party going on that you don't want to be at. Everyone is happy, laughing, drinking, dancing. It sounds like this (Invite everyone to make the sound of a wild, happy party). *Hamlet doesn't belong here. Hamlet, you are trying to avoid everyone. You aren't even pretending to be happy. But there is nowhere to hide. Every room in the castle is being used. Plus, you are the Prince of Denmark and people expect to see you here; you have duties.*

10. Now begin a sequence of activity in which you narrate Hamlet's passage through the castle:

Hamlet is trapped in a castle that is trying to be happy and expecting him to be so too. But he cannot be happy – he is still grieving for his father, he thinks his mother is wrong to marry Claudius. As he walks he thinks; thoughts he will share directly with us.

In preparation for this moment, write the following text from Hamlet's first major speech on large strips of paper on the wall around the room. Lead the group around the room in role as Hamlet to see, read and speak the words.

O that this too too solid flesh would melt

How weary, stale, flat and unprofitable,
Seem to me all the uses of this world!

That it should come to this!
But two months dead . . .

So excellent a king . . . so loving to my mother:
and yet, within a month . . . married with my uncle,

O, most wicked speed . . .

It is not nor it cannot come to good:

But break, my heart; for I must hold my tongue.

Give the group the opportunity to build upon this thinking and improvise Hamlet's further thinking.

11. On this journey around the castle he encounters a series of people: his uncle, the new king, his mother, a wedding guest, an old friend and finally, a peasant-servant. Remembering that we have already made pairs and allocated As and Bs, this sequence involves alternating between A and B as Hamlet and the *other* who he will encounter. Keep the group walking around the space until you announce each encounter.

   ● Hamlet meets a wedding guest: *As* are the guest, *Bs* are Hamlet. How do they look at each other? What does the guest think or feel about Hamlet? What does Hamlet think or feel? Watch some of these encounters. Now everyone move off – all are Hamlet.

   ● Hamlet meets his uncle, the new king: *Bs* are the king, *As* are Hamlet. How do they look at each other? What does the king think or feel about Hamlet? What does Hamlet think or feel? How is this communicated in an exchange of looks? Watch these. Now everyone move off – all are Hamlet.

   ● Hamlet meets his mother: *As* are the mother, *Bs* are Hamlet. How do they look at each other? What does the mother think or feel about Hamlet? What does Hamlet think or feel? What does she say to him? Watch these. Now everyone move off – all are Hamlet.

   ● Hamlet meets his friend Horatio: *As* are Horatio, *Bs* are Hamlet. How do they look at each other? What does Horatio think or feel about Hamlet? What does Hamlet think or feel? Watch these. Now everyone move off – all are Hamlet.

   ● Stop: Hamlet meets a peasant-villager: *As* are Hamlet, *Bs* are the peasant characters they created before (in the crypt); an outsider to the castle – you might not even recognise Hamlet. You come across Hamlet sitting on the floor in a lonely corner. (Is he crying?) Saying over and over, 'I must hold my tongue.' The servant stops to speak to him; to help him. What does the servant say? They have a conversation – five lines long.

   You might discuss how and why a peasant servant and a royal prince might speak to each other.

   These are the most developed scenes of the sequence. Prepare and watch these scenes.

   In a final moment, all are Hamlet again. End on the speaking of Hamlet's first soliloquy in unison.

12. Discuss the character of Hamlet with the group.

   What do you think about Hamlet? Even though he's a prince and was alive a long time ago, can you imagine what it's like to be him? In modern (or simple, human) terms he's struggling with two things: death and remarriage – things that lots of us might know something about. How do you think he might feel about his mother? His uncle? What do you think he should do? How much of his problem is because he is a prince? How might he feel?

Invite a student into the centre to give a tableau of Hamlet; sitting, head own, desolate. Invite other students to enter the circle and give him their best advice. Does he respond?

Phase 3: The ghost speaks

Part One: On the battlements

But listen: Hamlet's troubles have hardly begun. All of this is nothing to what is about to happen.

Castle Elsinore still stands today. It looks out across a narrow channel of water linking the cold North Sea and the freezing Baltic Sea. On a cold and stormy day it will be battered by frost-filled winds and driving rain. Today, when the next crucial scene occurs, is such a day. Hamlet climbs to a turret and then to a platform . . . to meet his fate!

To enhance the following scene, perhaps introduce the sound effect of an icy wind and the sea.

(Shouting over the sound effect!) A ghost has appeared to soldiers at midnight. They are terrified. The ghost looks like the dead king, Hamlet's father. The soldiers tell Horatio, Hamlet's friend, and Horatio tells Hamlet. He says he will meet them there that night . . . at midnight . . . to see if the ghost comes again.

Now ask for a few volunteers to mark out this scene in the centre of the circle.

Narrate:

The storm howls – the winds blow – the sea rolls – Hamlet steps out onto the turret with Horatio – and a soldier, Marcellus. Midnight strikes. The ghost enters. The soldiers are terrified. The ghosts raises a hand and beckons for Hamlet to follow him. They try to stop Hamlet going with the ghost. He goes. They follow.

13. Now reveal the text and place it around the acting space. Invite the group to make smaller groups and prepare to stage the scene. Suggest that the lines are quite simple and that they should try to learn them. Groups will perform the scenes with the sound effect in the background – so they will have to prepare to project!

Here is the edited scene:

Hamlet, Act 1, Scene IV

A storm blows.
Enter Hamlet, Horatio, and Marcellus.

Hamlet   The air bites shrewdly; it is very cold.

Horatio   Look, my lord, it comes!

Enter Ghost.

Hamlet   Angels and ministers of grace defend us!

Ghost beckons HAMLET

Hamlet   It will not speak; then I will follow it.

Horatio   Do not, my lord.

Hamlet   My fate cries out . . .
               Go on; I'll follow thee.

Exeunt Ghost and Hamlet.

Horatio*   Let's follow him.
Marcellus   Something is rotten in the state of Denmark.

Exeunt.

*This is Marcellus' line but we have re-assigned it for the sake of the edit.

Hamlet and the ghost

14. Discuss why the ghost might want Hamlet alone. Does he have something to tell him? What might it be?

   Now ask for volunteers to play Hamlet. Choose several and place them in the centre of a circle facing outwards. Explain that everyone else is going to be the ghost; so the outside circle will speak to the inside circle. Invite both groups to take up the physical stance of their character, ready for speaking. You will provide the words spoken by both characters (see below) and each character-group will repeat them out loud after you. You will offer the lines in a declamatory style and enjoy the heightened drama of the situation. Explain that we will do the scene several times – perhaps once for power and once for meaning and once as the full performance that you might even record to listen to later.

Hamlet, Act 1, Scene V

Enter Ghost and Hamlet

Hamlet	Speak; I'll go no further.
Ghost	Mark me.
Hamlet	I will.
Ghost	My hour is almost come…
Hamlet	Alas, poor ghost!
Ghost	I am thy father's spirit, Doom'd for a certain term to walk the night, And for the day confined to fast in fires, Till the foul crimes done in my days of nature Are burnt and purged away.
Hamlet	O God!
Ghost	Revenge his foul and most unnatural murder.
Hamlet	Murder!
Ghost	Murder most foul,
Hamlet	Haste me to know't,
Ghost	The serpent that did sting thy father's life Now wears his crown.
Hamlet	O my prophetic soul! My uncle!
Ghost	Sleeping within my orchard, …thy uncle stole,

... and in the porches of my ears did pour
The leperous distilment; (poison)
Thus was I, sleeping by a brother's hand ...
... If thou hast nature in thee, bear it not; ...
Adieu, adieu! Hamlet, remember me.

Exit Ghost.

Hamlet   O, Hold, hold, my heart;
... bear me stiffly up. Ay, thou poor ghost, ...
... O most pernicious woman!
O villain, villain, smiling, damned villain!

The time is out of joint: O cursed spite,
That ever I was born to set it right!

Ghost*   **(Whispering)** Remember me ... Revenge ... Swear it! ....

Exeunt

15. Discuss what has just been said by both characters. What has been revealed and what is expected to happen next? What words did you hear that you didn't understand? How do Shakespeare's words sound to our modern ears? Do you like his words? What makes them different? Special? What would you do next if you were Hamlet?

*You might like to note that tradition says that Shakespeare – an actor – might have played the ghost himself.

Part Two: The revenger's code

16. Discuss with the group: Why does the ghost ask Hamlet to take revenge ... rather than, for example, go to the police?

     The revenger's code is a tradition that comes from before the introduction of a proper legal system, one in which the courts punish people for doing wrong. Hamlet knows about the revenger's code and so does the ghost (and the audience) ... It will be a matter of shame for him not to act on it; it is a matter of honour. Someone has killed his father and he knows he should now take revenge ... but will he?

     Do you ever feel like taking revenge? Is it a natural thing to feel?

This is an important piece of historical exposition which helps to make sense of the story and Hamlet's dilemma. It will be useful to 'talk up' the idea of revenge and honour in order to understand the play and Hamlet's situation within it. You might expand the discussion into contemporary settings where revenge, honour killings or the like have power; these will probably be in more 'closed' communities on the margins of civil society – where the general authorities (police, courts) are excluded as a possible route for redress.

Tell the group: The two people who speak most clearly about revenge in the play are Laertes and Claudius the king. Later, when Laertes finds out his father has been killed he breaks into the king's throne room with his sword up and demands revenge. He says, '*O though vile king, give me my father... I'll not be juggled with... I'll be revenged most thoroughly...!*' and the king encourages him, saying, '*Where the offence is, let the great axe fall.*'

Ask the class: What do you think Hamlet does next? Would you like to find out? We are going to look at the whole of the rest of the play...

Phase 4: The whole story

17. In some ways the play is as much about Hamlet's thinking along the way to revenge, than it is about the tragic narrative... but here we look at the broad sweep of the story. It is told in the form of a 'story whoosh!' – the instant story technique beloved of drama specialists. Here is a simplified version of the narrative with a sprinkling of Shakespearean text.

Hamlet: a story whoosh!

For the intiated, the *Story Whoosh!* is a great technique for instantly summoning a story before the group. Whereas other techniques might bring us into consideration of the details of a story, the *Story Whoosh!* allows us to focus on the broad sweep of the whole story. The group stands in a wide circle and you tell the story concentrating on characters, situations and settings. As you mention each item, you invite a student or *group* of students to enter the circle and create a tableau of the person or item mentioned. At the end of each short 'chapter' of the story wave your hand over the circle and call 'Whoosh!' This is the signal for the stage to be cleared, students to return to their places and the next chapter to be built.

In Denmark, by the shore of the cold North Sea, stands a castle: Elsinore, the home of young Prince Hamlet. Hamlet's mother marries his uncle soon after his father death. The uncle is crowned king. Hamlet still mourns his father's death and hates, rejects, despises the marriage.

'But break my heart for I must hold my tongue' **Whoosh!**

At the castle turrets stand guards. They have seen a ghost; the ghost of the dead king, Hamlet's father. They call for Hamlet to come the next night. The ghost appears and tells Hamlet that he was murdered by his own brother who is now the king – poisoned through the ear as he lay in the orchard. Hamlet must take revenge!

'Revenge this foul and most unnatural murder!' **Whoosh!**

Hamlet delays in the revenge; he doesn't carry out the murder of the king straight away. Weeks later Claudius still rules Denmark with Hamlet's mother by his side. Perhaps Hamlet doesn't trust the ghost . . . he could be an evil demon and lying! Perhaps he is too clever for his own good and thinks too much! Perhaps he struggles with the revenger's code – in the bible god says, 'Vengeance is mine!'

'What a piece of work is man?' **Whoosh!**

Claudius the king is suspicious of Hamlet; his mother worried. They pay two of Hamlet's friends, Rosencrantz and Guildenstern, to spy on him. He realises they are spying for the king. He acts as if he were mad.

'Though this be madness, yet there is method in it.' **Whoosh!**

A troupe of actors arrive. Hamlet decides to use them to try and trick the king into showing his guilt – that he DID kill the king. They are to perform a play in which a king is killed in the orchard with poison through his ear! Will the king react?

'The play's the thing, wherein I'll catch the conscience of the king.' **Whoosh!**

Hamlet meets his old girlfriend, Ophelia. He tells her he never really loved her and that she should never get married. She is broken-hearted.

'Get thee to a nunnery!' **Whoosh!**

The play is performed. Everyone sees the murder in the orchard acted out. The king shouts to end the play. *'Lights! Lights!'* Hamlet follows the king and finds him praying for forgiveness. He draws his sword to carry out the killing, but stops. If he kills him whilst he is praying he'll go to heaven . . . and Hamlet wants him to go to hell! He doesn't kill him.

    'Now I might do it, pat . . . ' **Whoosh!**

Gertrude, Hamlet's mother, decides to speak to him. Old Polonius – Ophelia's father – hides behind a curtain to spy on them. Hamlet argues with his mother, the ghost returns, Hamlet thinks it is the king behind the curtain and stabs at it – killing Polonius. Hamlet hides his body.

    'O what a rash and bloody deed is this!' **Whoosh!**

The king now knows that Hamlet knows that he killed his father and plots against him. He sends him to England with Rosencrantz and Guildenstern, with a secret note asking the king of England to kill him. Hamlet switches the notes and Rosencrantz and Guildenstern are killed instead.

    On his way back – determined to finally kill the king – Hamlet meets the gravedigger.

    'Alas, poor, Yorick!' **Whoosh!**

Hamlet's ex-girlfriend Ophelia drowns herself in despair; she has lost Hamlet and Polonius, her father! Her brother, Laertes, must now take revenge on Hamlet! The king plots to use Laertes to make sure Hamlet is killed. Laertes doesn't delay in taking HIS revenge!

    'My revenge will come!' **Whoosh!**

Laertes and Hamlet are to fight a *friendly* duel with swords in front of the king and queen. The king poisons Laertes sword so that the slightest cut will kill Hamlet. Just in case, he also poisons the cup of wine that he says the winner will drink. They fight. Laertes nicks Hamlet with the poison sword and he begins to die. The queen drinks the poison wine and begins to die. Hamlet kills Laertes. Finally, Hamlet stabs the king. Hamlet dies.

    'Now cracks a noble heart. Goodnight, Sweet Prince.
    And flights of angels sing thee to thy rest.' **Whoosh!**

Discuss the broad sweep of the narrative and students' responses to it. What questions do they have? Propose that we now look in detail at some elements of the play.

Phase 5: The Royal House of Denmark

Part One: The queen: did she know?

18. Ask the class: What do we know about the queen, Gertrude? Or what possibilities can we imagine about her? Or what questions do you have about her? Write each fact or idea down on scraps of paper. Gather all this information together around a representative object such as the crown.

    What questions would you ask her if you could? Perhaps why she married so soon? Why she married her husband's brother? Did she know about the murder? This seems like the key question. It's possible that she never knew about it and dies without knowing. Or you might think that she knew all along and may even have been part of the plot to kill the old king. Or, at least, that she is guilty of allowing herself to be 'strung along' by Claudius. There might be a political story to tell: as a woman, does she need to marry quickly in order to hold onto her crown? Would she otherwise be slung on the scrapheap after the old king's death?

    Note: We don't know from the play with any real clarity whether Gertrude knew about the murder or not ... but it is safe to assume she didn't. Why she married so quickly, and against the wishes of her son is perhaps a puzzle. At the very least, is it thoughtless towards Hamlet? This space in the characterisation (as so often with Shakespeare) allows room for our speculations and imaginings.

19. Teacher-in-role: Gertrude. Explain that you are going to take on the character of the queen and answer their questions.

    Think through your role: How deep is your guilt? Have you married for love or to protect your position as queen? Did the country need a strong king? Perhaps you thought Hamlet wasn't ready yet. What are you hiding?

    In your characterisation here, it is interesting and useful to present a character who isn't clear cut – a problematic, uncertain character. Or even, to contradict the group's expectations.

    But don't forget that you are also still the queen and can refuse to answer these commoner's questions – you might avoid some questions by becoming uppity and irritated.

Part Two: The king's guilt

20. Discussion: What about Claudius? Run a briefer process of collecting facts. What do we know about him? What questions do we have about him?

    This time we're going to send him down his own castle corridor; at the end of which is his throne room. The walls of the corridor echo with all the words ever spoken about him and the old king. One side speaks the words he WANTS to hear and other side the SECRET things that people say about him behind his back. When he gets to the end of the corridor he will enter his throne room and sit upon his throne. How will he sit upon it? What will he say or think when he does so?

Explain that the sequence could be run as many times as you like with a new king each time and people deciding which side they would like to be on. This is a developed version of a technique sometimes called a 'conscience alley'. You might invite the group to form pairs and to decide upon their opposing statements together – they will stand opposite each other in our long corridor.

21. Now introduce some of Shakespeare's text as given to Claudius at his low point of guilt; at the point at which he tries to pray and reveals to us (the audience) that he DID kill the old king. Write the text on strips of paper and lay it on the floor along the 'corridor'. Have Claudius speak the lines as the walls 'speak' to him.

King Claudius' speech

O, my offence is rank; it smells to heaven;
A brother's murder.

... this cursed hand ... thicker than itself with brother's blood,

Is there not rain enough in the sweet heavens
To wash it white as snow?

'Forgive me my foul murder'?
That cannot be;

since I am still possess'd
Of those effects for which I did the murder,
My crown, mine own ambition and my queen.

O wretched state! O bosom black as death!
Help, angels! Bow, stubborn knees

Discuss the meaning and impact of the text. What does it reveal about Claudius?

22. Now place the two elements – speaking walls and text – together and work towards a more performative presentation. You might make a sound recording of the final sequence.

    The final time you perform seat the king in his throne and invite students in the 'walls' to step behind Claudius and 'thought-track' him – placing a hand on his shoulder and speaking his thoughts.

Part Three: The Royal House of Denmark: chain-tracking

23. Announce to the group: Having considered each royal character in turn, we are going to think about three moments in the story and bring them to life in a special way – allowing the characters to speak **new** text and create our own **new** scenes.

    Explain the process. We will make a tableau of each moment using three actors. We will then invite others to enter the scene and speak as the characters by laying a hand gently on their shoulder and speaking. Others will add lines progressively to the character's speeches by placing a hand on the last speaker's shoulder and forming a 'chain' attached to each royal personage. The characters are IN the moment but speaking their private thoughts directly to the audience.

    Below are three key moments from the narrative. You might decide to explore just one moment in greater depth. They are:

- The start of the play: the marriage and coronation have just happened and Hamlet is skulking miserably.
- The middle of the play: Hamlet knows about the murder and is acting mad, Claudius and Gertrude watch him.
- The end of the play: Gertrude has drunk the poison intended for Hamlet, Hamlet has been stabbed and has stabbed Claudius . . . all on their last legs!

At the end of the spoken monologues formed from the 'chain-tracking' invite the actors to write down the line they have created and put these together to form a continuous soliloquy. You might display these and ask the first actor to read them all as a single speech – the playwrights see their lines spoken by an actor!

What do these new scenes reveal about the characters and their situation?

Phase 6: To be or not to be

24. Hamlet's most famous speech – which is probably the most famous speech in the whole of the English language – is usually considered a reflection on suicide. The very first question, 'To be or not to be' might be read as 'to live or not to live'. Discuss this. Propose that you now look at an edited version of this speech. (Feel free to tackle the whole speech, if you prefer). Look at the speech together and uncover its meaning. Some words will need explanation.

The Speech: To be or not to be

> To be, or not to be, that is the question:
> Whether 'tis nobler in the mind to suffer
> The slings and arrows of outrageous fortune
> Or to take arms against a sea of troubles
> And by opposing end them. To die, to sleep
> No more . . .
> To sleep – perchance to dream: ay, there's the rub,
> For in that sleep of death what dreams may come
> When we have shuffled off this mortal coil,
> Must give us pause.

25. Having explored the speech, propose that the group learn it as a piece of actor's text. Suggest that there is a satisfaction and pleasure in simply mastering such a famous and iconic speech.

    In the further development, think about how the speech might be spoken by your whole group. Experiment with the techniques of choral speaking, and perhaps work towards a performance – either in a public setting or for audio recording.

    You might like to discuss *wider* meanings of the 'To be' speech; does it just mean dying or does 'being' mean more to be a full person, for example? Edward Bond says that 'To be or not to be' is the question children ask everyday. What does he mean?

Phase 7: Ophelia's story

Part One: Her story, her problems

26. Ophelia is a very interesting character who allows us to look at the patriarchal world of the play and ask some questions about her role and her life.

   Ophelia is Hamlet's *girlfriend* at the start of the play, but by the end she has lost her mind, her love (who has killed her father) and her father, Polonius. Some would say she is a victim of all of the men around her; that she dies to escape from a situation she feels she is trapped in and can't change. In this next section, we are going to look at Ophelia's story.

   Note: You might like to show the Millais' image of Ophelia's death to develop the group's response.

   The 'character whoosh!' is a phrase coined to describe a version of a story whoosh! but focusing on just one character in order to look in detail at his/her story. Look now at Ophelia's story.

Ophelia: A character whoosh!

Ophelia is a gentle-woman of the royal court of Denmark; her home Elsinore Castle. Her father is an old advisor to the king; his name, Polonius. Her brother, a proud gentleman of court, is Laertes. We do not know anything about her mother. At the start of the play Laertes is about to leave Elsinore and together with Polonius, warns Ophelia about Hamlet – her boyfriend; they say that because Hamlet is a prince he can't do what he likes and should not be trusted. They **control** her. *Whoosh!*

After Hamlet has seen the ghost and begun to act mad he visits Ophelia and just stares at her. She is **disturbed** and she tells her father, Polonius, that she thinks Hamlet has gone mad. Polonius thinks Hamlet is lovesick because Ophelia has been ignoring him as her father had told her to. Polonius tells the king. *Whoosh!*

Polonius and Claudius the king hide to secretly listen in on Ophelia's next meeting with Hamlet. They tell her to return his love-letters. Hamlet is cruel and aggressive to Ophelia telling her to never get married, but join a convent saying, 'Get thee to a nunnery!' He **abuses** her. Thinking he is completely mad Ophelia says, 'O what a noble mind is here overthrown!' (Invite all to repeat). *Whoosh!*

Ophelia sits with Hamlet whilst the play intended to trick the king is acted out. Hamlet **mocks** and is cruel to her again. "Lights! Lights!" ***Whoosh!***

We next see Ophelia after her father has been killed mistakenly by Hamlet. She is losing her mind. She sings rude, crazy songs. When Laertes, her brother, returns he sees that she is **broken**. She has gone completely mad, handing out flowers and lost in her own world. ***Whoosh!***

The queen, Gertrude, reports that Ophelia has **drowned**; she has fallen from a branch of a willow tree into a stream and been dragged down by the weight of her dresses. A priest will later say that she may have killed herself. ***Whoosh!***

At her funeral, Laertes jumps into the grave to hold her one last time, Hamlet sees this and they fight in the grave over who loved her most. Laertes blames Hamlet for her death. ***Whoosh!***

Discuss the character and her life. What does the group feel about her? Whose fault is her death? How might you summarise her life through the play?

To take out a word from each episode of the ***Whoosh!*** we might say:

- **Controlled**
- **Disturbed**
- **Abused**
- **Mocked**
- **Broken**
- **Drowned**

This sequence of words might summarise her life and seems to reveal the depth of her struggles and unhappiness. Does the group agree with the list?

27. Suggest bringing this sequence of words to life as a way of capturing Ophelia's life. Invite volunteers into the circle to realise each of the words in tableau as you speak them. Alternatively, break into six groups and give a little time for preparation of images to capture the sense of each moment represented by the words. Then invite the groups into the circle in order. Music might enhance the feel of this moment.

Invite a discussion: how does the group feel about her? Should she have been stronger? Was she a victim of the men and the court? Why do her family warn her of Hamlet so much? Does she suffer from not having a mother around? How? What makes her go mad? How does she feel when Hamlet is so vicious to her? Did she kill herself or die by accident? As the only two women in the story, how do Ophelia and Gertrude offer images of women? Would Gertrude lie about Ophelia's death to protect her memory? What could Ophelia have done differently? What would you want to say to her or to the people (the men) in her life?

28. To go deeper into the text, assign groups sections of edited text for preparation and performance:

- Ophelia's first meeting with her father and brother, (Act 1, Scene III)
- Hamlet's terrible attack on her – 'Get thee to a nunnery', (Act 3, Scene I) and
- The scene of Ophelia's descent into madness (Act 4, Scene V).

Copies of the scenes can be found online and either yourself – or students – can produce your own tailored edits. This is an interesting exercise in reading for meaning and editing for clarity.

Part Two: Ophelia's death

The first witness: Shakespeare's poetry

We know that Ophelia's life ends in tragedy. We know she has gone mad – singing crude songs and collecting flowers. Soon after Laertes, her brother, sees her again, Queen Gertrude comes to tell of her death. She says that Ophelia had made a garland out of weeds and climbed onto a willow tree that hangs over a stream to hang it on a branch. The branch had broken and Ophelia fell into the stream. She floated there for a while – held up like a mermaid by the air in her dresses. But as her dresses became weighed down with water she was dragged under... without struggling... and drowned.

29. Consider Shakespeare's description of this. We have simplified the speech a little for accessibility's sake, but you might like to use the whole speech. Look at the piece together initially and discuss meaning and imagery.

Ophelia's death

1.

There is a willow grows aslant a brook, (slanting over)
That shows his leaves in the glassy stream;

2.
There with fantastic garlands did she come
Of crow-flowers, nettles, daisies, and long purples... (various weeds)
3.
There, on the pendent boughs her coronet weeds (boughs – branches)
Clambering to hang, an envious sliver broke; (sliver – small part of branch)
4.
When down her weedy trophies and herself
Fell in the weeping brook. Her clothes spread wide;
5.
And, mermaid-like, awhile they bore her up: (held her up for a time)
Which time she chanted snatches of old tunes; (she sang bits of old tunes)
6.
As one incapable of her own distress, (she didn't know she was drowning)
Or like a creature native and indued (like a creature that lives in water)
Unto that element:
7.
but long it could not be
Till that her garments, heavy with their drink, (her clothes heavy with water)
8.
Pull'd the poor wretch from her melodious lay (she had been laying flat and singing)
To muddy death.

30. Explain that the speech is broken into eight numbered parts. The class will form eight new groups and each one will get one of the lines. Each group will think about what it means and how to speak the lines as a group to achieve maximum dramatic impact. We will then put all of the pieces back together and perform them as one... perhaps making an audio recording.

    Allow time for this preparation to happen.

    Bring the group together and perform the speech.

    Afterwards, discuss the speech; what lines are most memorable? What lines or words do you like? How does Shakespeare make something terrible (a drowning) sound beautiful? Why does he do this for Ophelia?

The second witness: your poetry

31. In this exercise, we shall be trying our hand at writing our own descriptive dramatic language. Imagine that there was a second witness to Ophelia's death – perhaps a servant (or villager). Gertrude wishes to make a terrible death seem beautiful. You were also a witness to the drowning… what is your account? If you were to write your own version of Ophelia's death what would *you* write? How would you make it sound? Still beautiful? Or something else? More terrible? More realistic? More truthful? Think about adjectives in particular and adding them in interesting ways. What effect do you wish to have on your audience?

    Use Shakespeare's speech as a model for some original performance poetry. Invite students to think about the possible impacts of lyrical dramatic language and how to achieve this.

    Prepare and perform.

Phase 8: The final scene: a royal massacre

And so we come to the final moments of the play – as anticipated in our initial meeting with the gravedigger. In this section, we will attempt a full theatrical presentation of this intricate, climactic scene.

Firstly, as a way of recapping, enact the final, deadly moments of action in the style of a story whoosh! Take it slowly and carefully.

> *Claudius, conniving as ever, has arranged it so that Laertes challenges Hamlet to a friendly fencing match in which Laertes' sword will be poisoned. But the match becomes deadly. Claudius also poisons Hamlet's drink… just in case he wins the fight. But Gertrude drinks the poisoned cup and dies. Poisoned swords are swapped, Laertes and Hamlet are stabbed with the same poisoned sword. They begin to die. Laertes reveals the truth about the king and (finally) Hamlet kills Claudius.*

32. Discuss the key actions and take responses.

    Propose that we prepare to enact this scene – with an edited version of Shakespeare's text – including the swordfight. The obvious problem will be the nature of the fight. Without years of training this will call for some creative but safe solutions. For example, the stylisation of the fight, in which the audience are given a sense of the murderous aggression but without suggesting that it is a real event. Well-realised, this turns out to be more dramatically effective than an inexpert stage fight. The degree to which this action scene is realised on the stage can be determined by yourself and the group.

Groups will need to cast the scene, decide on the movement needed (called 'blocking'), learn the simple lines and prepare.

Note: You might enhance the final performances by creating a clearly defined stage space and items of furniture – indicating two thrones – might be important.

This is the first time in the scheme that we have thought directly about the 'blocking' of a scene; we find ourselves in the final stages in a wholly theatrical world working towards a simple performance. We have been on all sorts of excursions with characters and ideas but find ourselves now back in the theatre world that gave the story its sense in the first place; *Hamlet* is a play for acting.

Hamlet, Act 5, Scene II: The final scene

Hamlet   The readiness is all.

Enter King Claudius, Queen Gertrude, Laertes, Lords, Osric, and Attendants with foils (rapiers)

Hamlet   **(to Laertes)** Give me your pardon, sir: I've done you wrong;

(They shake hands)

Hamlet   Give us the foils.

They prepare to fight.

Laertes   Come, my lord.

They fight. Hamlet hits Laertes.

Osric   A hit, a very palpable hit.
King Claudius Give him the cup.
                  HamletI'll play this bout first

They fight.

Queen Gertrude	The queen carouses* to thy fortune, Hamlet. (*drinks)
King Claudius	Gertrude, do not drink.
King Claudius	[Aside] It is the poison'd cup: it is too late.

Laertes	Have at you now!

Laertes wounds Hamlet; then in scuffling, they exchange rapiers. A genuine fight ensues and Hamlet wounds Laertes with the poisoned sword.

King Claudius	Part them.
Hamlet	Nay, come, again.

QUEEN GERTRUDE falls

Queen Gertrude	The drink, the drink! I am poison'd.

Dies

Hamlet	O villany! Treachery! Seek it out.
Laertes	It is here, Hamlet: Hamlet, thou art slain;
	The king, the king's to blame.
Hamlet	Then, venom, to thy work.

Stabs King Claudius.

All	Treason! treason!

King Claudius dies.

Laertes	He is justly served;

Dies

Hamlet	Horatio, I am dead;
	Thou livest; report me
	The rest is silence.

Dies

Horatio   Now cracks a noble heart. Good night sweet prince
                And flights of angels sing thee to thy rest!

A solemn drum.

The End.

Phase 9: Assessment task

33. We have had great results over recent years with a distinctive form of summative play-making at the end of our Shakespeare schemes. This has involved a devising process in which students are invited to work within the world of Shakespeare's play but to create their own reassembling of the characters and narratives in original forms. In the dramatic montages that result, we will hear Shakespeare's text spoken but alongside text which might have been created during the process of our drama explorations. A group might choose to look at Ophelia or Claudius, or at levels of deceit, or guilt, or madness, or death, or at royalty through the eyes of a servant. Each group will develop their own perspective on the play and create their own compelling pieces, standing, as they say, on the shoulders of giants.

Year 10/11 scheme: *Extreme*

This scheme of work sets out to explore the issue of terrorism in a contained and protected way. Its key point of exploration is the place of history in a community's identity and in particular the sense of historic oppression and injustice that might fuel extreme human action.

It takes the troubles in Northern Ireland as its example and setting. This is my own area of knowledge and family experience. A colleague has chosen to set the same events against the background of Palestine, making necessary adjustments. Clearly, the issue of international 'Islamic' terrorism is markedly different to the Irish example but the sense of 'my people's living history' is perhaps an aspect. Discussion of the 'Irish problem' (a problem that has begun to resolve itself since the scheme was first developed) now offers us a level of protection behind which the 'hot' questions about the current state of our world can be approached.

The investigation allows students to explore their own responses to the situation.

The chief drama focus is the idea of 'building belief' in objects and situations.

The scheme leads students towards a research-based practical assessment. The assessment details are included.

Phase 1: Discussion and personal input

1. Open a general discussion: What is 'terror'? Have you ever felt terror? When? The group share their personal stories. You share yours. They don't need to be terrorism-related, of course; getting lost in a shopping centre as a child might be enough. Why might someone want to make you feel 'terror' on purpose? Open this out to a much wider discussion taking in recent history. Does somebody want to fill 'us' with terror? Perhaps they want to make us fearful more than they want to kill us? Or does someone want to kill us? Why? Who is the 'us' in that statement? Reflect upon those sets of

numbers '9/11' and '7/7' and other events that might hold significance in your own place. Why do these things happen?

The scheme was first taught in Manchester and refers for a short time to the 'Manchester bomb' when in 1996 the IRA detonated a car bomb in the centre of Manchester on a busy Saturday afternoon. Full warning was given and no-one was killed. However, property was destroyed or severely damaged (including the Royal Exchange Theatre) and has since been rebuilt.

The bomb forms a small part of Manchester's social memory and still today when students are asked the questions below they can tell stories that are part of their family's history. In a very important way they demonstrate the concept of a community's 'living history' and how it might help to cement their identity.

In other circumstances it may be necessary to alter the focus of this discussion. Perhaps there are instances in your own community's recent past which might be explored. Alternatively, make this a very personal exploration a discussion of 'Where were you (or your family) when the towers were hit? How did you find out about it? In this case you will introduce the idea of the Irish troubles at a slightly later point and tell the story of the Manchester bomb as a starting point.

The following is how the scheme has been begun with a specific group in its original setting. You will make your own adjustments.

Phase 2: The Manchester bomb

Part One: Creating the scene

2. You begin: You might not remember this yourself but your families may... In 1996 a bomb was planted in Manchester and set off one Saturday afternoon when people were out shopping. What can you tell me about it? What do you know about your family on that day? Why does someone want to cause you terror? Who planted it? Why did they give a warning? How do you give a warning? Discuss predetermined code words between the police and IRA. Encourage a general discussion which outlines the history of Northern Ireland.

3. Create a whole group tableaux. Describe the scene. Integrate information from the previous discussion if possible. ('My gran worked in Woolworths, she had to clear out the customers.' Etc.) As the warning was given people were told to evacuate the area. As they did so we imagine that a panic

ensued. A surge of people moved quickly away from Cross Street and the bomb. They felt 'terror'. A photographer happened to be there to capture this moment. The photographer was stood looking into the crowd as it moves quickly forward. The resulting photo would be broadcast across the world. It captured the feeling of panic and 'terror'. You can find this photograph – amongst many others – with a quick internet search. You might then display it as large as possible on a blank wall.

Note: In pre-internet days we worked this section without ever seeing the photograph; we created it as an act of imagination. You might find that this is still your best option.

Either way, we are going to recreate it. It is essential to 'build belief'; to capture the reality of the terror.

Process:

- Indicate a line which is the furthest point forward that the crowd can come.
- The crowd must give the sense of moving forward in panic.
- Prepare students to adopt a specific character. Are they trying to keep hold of a child's hand? Falling beneath the crush out of weakness? Pushing another out of the way?
- Students come forward to the line one at a time. They build upon the tableaux offered by others. It should not be a single line but a 'knot' of people.
- Once the photograph is constructed you, as the observer/photographer check its reality. Challenge minute details to get it right. 'Terror' is what we should see.
- Now you are looking for the 'sound' of terror. At your signal your students must give the sound that accompanies the picture. Expect to have a number of failed attempts which do not satisfy your insistence on reality and belief.
- Ask the class to close their eyes whilst you close yours. Listen to the sound again.
- 'Spot-light' individual shouts amidst the chaotic sound. Look for full emotional commitment.
- Give a final performance. 'This is the sound of terror'.
- Complete the moment with a summary 'root sentence' exercise: 'The streets of Manchester, streets of . . .', inviting a range of responses.
- Now show a second picture of the devastated street after the bomb. A red letter box stands undamaged. Discuss the picture.

4. Focus directly on the idea of 'building belief' and why it matters. If we cannot make an audience believe in the reality of certain key objects we limit the effectiveness of our dramas. We have to be able to give an object, a situation, a character real dramatic value.

    The bomb planted in Manchester came from somewhere. It was assembled in a house somewhere not far from the centre of Manchester. It was transported in the white van which exploded with the detonation. If you don't believe in my bomb you will not believe in my story.

    An exercise: In the centre of the circle is a small box. It is filled with a quantity of high explosives that will destroy this room and building. How are we to treat it? Approach it? Touch it? How we do these things will determine whether the 'audience' is willing to believe it is a bomb. Students are invited, one at a time, to enter the circle and have the task of arming the bomb. All they have to do is enter the room, approach the device, join two wires and punch in a detonating time. Try it several times and pick out 'best practice'. Expect this to focus on patterns of breathing, slowness of movement, the delicacy and tremble of hands. We should become super-aware of slight indicators of tension. What does it take to build belief? Now we put it into action.

    You might like to introduce the concept of 'cathexis'. This is a term borrowed (we think) from psychoanalysis which describes a process through which an object is imbued with symbolic meaning. In stage terms, Edward Bond has used the term to describe the process through which objects on a stage are imbued with great symbolic and theatrical meaning. Our 'building belief' in the bomb is a simple version of the process. In this initial task, the audience is brought to accept its reality as a deadly device. In more advanced forms of cathexis, the object would be imbued with symbolic meaning, e.g. the red pillar box could become a symbol of the people's resilience, the bomb a symbol of the terrorist's latent and destructive anger.

    To develop this line of thought further, propose at the end of the enactment: I know this is a bomb, I believe it... you have made it *live* for me. But this bomb is something else as well... perhaps it is a symbol of a people's rage. If I were the person who planted it I could name it such, 'This bomb is my silent rage waiting to erupt in violence'. What might YOU name it? Invite responses.

Part Two: The cell

Small group play-making

5.   We are going to try and get closer to these people and why they do these
     things. They must have been somewhere close by in Manchester with the
     bomb. Perhaps in a house. Planning. Waiting. Assembling. Just before they
     left the house they armed the bomb. This action, which you have just
     attempted, must be a part of the drama you are going to create.

     Again, our intention will be to build belief in this group of people. There
     are two things to consider about groups of individuals which will make the
     group realistic: i. delineating characters and ii. exposing the group's social
     structure.

i.   Who makes up this group of people? Just as in life no two people are
     identical. Calling the group 'terrorists' doesn't tell us everything we need
     to know about them. Introduce the idea of 'character delineation'; making
     the members of a group separate individuals with different feelings,
     motivations and reactions. It should be possible for the audience to gain
     a clear idea of each character's reasons – or 'motivation' for being a
     'terrorist'. The exposition of motivation should be revealed subtly.

ii. Introduce or recap the concept of 'status'. Human beings are social
     creatures and tend to arrange themselves into social hierarchies when
     placed together. Through verbal and non-verbal means of communi-
     cation we negotiate a 'pecking order' within our groups. To show a
     'realistic' group of people we have to capture this negotiation of status
     in our presentation of the group. Many of the conflicts between people
     we explore in drama are negotiations of status. In the case of this group
     of 'terrorists' the situation may be even more extreme and the tensions
     heightened. The IRA is an 'army' and organised along military structures;
     there will probably be a 'captain' of this cell, perhaps experts in various
     necessary fields with differing levels of importance. The second aspect
     that might heighten the human relationships is secrecy. It is illegal to
     even belong to this group. They are planning a potentially murderous
     act of violence and must preserve its secrecy. In these circumstances
     we might expect that discipline between the members of the group
     would be high. As would tensions.

Ask your group to produce a piece of drama which shows this group during
their last moments of preparation before leaving their flat for the bombing.

This group must be presented as realistically as possible. Some useful questions to ask:

i.   Do all of the group know that this bombing is intended to not kill?
ii. Are all of the group comfortable with the bombing of a busy public street?
iii. Are all members of the group here willingly?
iv. Are all members of the group members of the IRA 'cell' or hired for a particular job?
v.   Would accents be of use? How do we achieve this without a comic effect?

The groups form and prepare.
    Watch. Discuss the motivations shown. What has been revealed about the people depicted? Discuss 'good dramatic practice'.

From a purely dramatic point of view this section of the work is a very valuable exploration of how to create a sense of reality in the presentation of groups and private motivations. That we do so under a moment of extreme stress and tension only heightens the possibilities.

Part Three: Whole group street scene

6. Return to the earlier whole group street scene. As the terrorists leave their flat at the end of the last scene we are almost back at this moment. But we're not there yet. We are going to explore a moment which did not happen in the real event. But the moment is one which will test the character, commitment and motivation of the terrorist.
    Look again at the tableau (either the photo or the one we created ourselves). Who are these people and where were they three minutes earlier? We are going to build a tableau of this ordinary Saturday afternoon, in Manchester city centre. No one in the scene as it begins has any notion of the bomb except, of course, for the terrorists. They have parked the white van on Cross Street and walked away from it.
    We shall clear the space and enter into a whole group tableau one at a time to create the full scene. There may be families, teenagers, market stall holders, security or police officers, plus, a mother with a young child, etc. You might identify which shops are adjacent to the space, benches, dustbins, etc.

We build the scene and bring it to life, spotlighting the different elements of the scene and building up a gentle belief in the situation. Stop.

The terrorists are watching. Imagine that the detonation will take place with a mobile phone. The 'number' of the bomb's detonation device is already in the mobile screen. The number only needs 'sending' to cause the explosion. The terrorist charged with detonation is watching at a safe distance. Are people suspicious? How does he/she feel as he/she watches the scene? How do they respond to the people they are putting in danger? There are families, children, here. Thought-track his/her thoughts.

Freeze the action.

We hear the terrorists telephone a warning to police. They give the code name which tells the police that this is a genuine bomb warning. The security officer in the scene receives a radio alert. He/she begins to move people towards the end of the street. A panic ensues. The crowd move quickly away. The street is cleared. This is as planned by the cell.
   A young child is separated from its parents. It is alone and unseen on the deserted street. It finds an abandoned children's fast food meal besides the white van. It stays to eat it. The terrorist holds the mobile phone with which to detonate or disarm the bomb. They are watching the child. The time is due at which they must detonate. They have orders, they are disciplined, they will be judged on the success of this mission. Will they do it? How do they feel about the child? Is it the enemy? By not detonating at the appointed time (say, 11.00am on the dot) they may jeopardise their own position. If they do not detonate to save the child, or if they reveal themselves in order to save the child they may sacrifice themselves. It is five seconds to 11am. The child is sitting by the car on the empty street.

Invite students to spontaneously improvise their solutions to this problem. Forum the possibilities. Discuss the outcomes. What do the different possibilities tell us about the state of mind of the terrorist? Can this highly motivated and highly disciplined 'soldier' have their 'humanity' awakened by the presence of the child? Or is this a fantasy? How different might it be if the motivation was religious and not largely political?
   Build towards a final performance of the scene which is the culmination of the group's thoughts.

Part Four: The terrorist

Writing in role: chain monologue

7. Tell the group: We are going to slow down our work and, in particular, our thinking about the mind of the terrorist. Sit the class in threes, each with their own blank piece of paper and pen. The groups of three are going to work together to write monologues (or poetry) from the mind of the terrorist at the moment we have just reached in the narrative.

    The process is simple:

- The group is given silent 'thinking' time. They each need to tune themselves into the character's mind at the moment explored earlier. As a writer they need to consider an opening line for a monologue or 'dramatic' poem. An opening line must have impact.
- After the moment of thought, the first person in the group writes their opening line.
- The papers are then passed to the right to the next person.
- The 'receiver' of the paper reads the line. There is a period of thinking time and they then add the second line. This is then passed to the right again.
- The process continues for three or four rotations until the papers arrive back for the final time at the originating 'writer'.
- You might play music to enhance the moment and, when not working, students might close their eyes or even lie down until their turn comes around.
- The writers then have to prepare to perform their monologue/poem.
- Performance.

> It is useful to point out to students the great difference ordinarily between language that is improvised and language that is written. The process of 'writing' tends to be a slower process. The intervention of the pen and the action of writing, at the very least, 'slows down' the mental process of creation. It makes developing dramatic structures within a monologue and the use of heightened language more likely and more effective. Having said that, students coming to dramatic writing for the first time will often struggle to create a flow of ideas which can sustain an effective monologue. This is where the strength of the 'chain monologue' becomes evident. By establishing a situation whereby each thought is extended,

augmented or perhaps challenged by a second, and then a third, contributing 'mind' we create a stream of freshly imaginative responses. At the same time, the originating minds maintain ownership of their own imaginative product.

Explain: We have really come to explore the minds of this group of people and the community to which they belong. Let's summarise. Who are these people? Where do they come from? What is their community like; their family? Gather together a brief history of Northern Ireland and the 'Troubles', filling in where necessary. Discuss how a people's 'History' might be carried with them into their daily lives. How they might live with things on a daily basis which happened perhaps even hundreds of years before they were born. These stories that their community tell become part of their identity... of who they are. The stories build a perception of long-term injustice and loss. The community might share this feeling very strongly. It draws them together as a people.

Phase 3: The community

Part One: The culture

The cultural and musical history of Ireland can give us entry to the powerful feelings of its people. In this scheme we use two songs. 'Green Isle' is a Ewan McColl song that traces a thousand years of oppression. I use the version recorded by Christy Moore. It is a bare and tender version with a distinctive Irish voice. The second song, 'My Youngest Son Came Home Today' is another McColl song about the return of the body of a young Irish 'soldier' to his Belfast family. The song offers us a situation and the beginnings of a community of characters who will become the characters of the next phase of the drama.

For this second song we have worked with an idea from Jonothan Neelands who suggested the powerful dramatic impact of live singing during student performances. It is true. I introduce this idea to the group by singing the song to the class myself. If you don't want to perform the song yourself I have also used Billy Bragg's version of the song, readily available online.

As an accompaniment to the song and to secure a sense of reality we have developed a simple power-point presentation of images. The images were gained from an internet image search. This is a highly effective and easily accessible supplement to the drama work.

The presentation used currently includes:

- a selection of photographs of the aftermath of the Manchester bomb
- a map of the island of Ireland with Northern Ireland marked clearly and Belfast pinpointed
- Belfast streets, terraced housing
- a masked gunman
- documentary photographs of a funeral procession through the streets
- shots of the grieving family
- shots of a masked gunman firing a volley over the coffin
- shots of end-of-terrace murals: military, aggressive, incendiary; 'History is written by the victors'
- a child standing with a toy gun, advancing on the camera. Behind him in large graffiti letters: BASTARDS.

Part Two: Becoming the community

Song and image stimulus: Green Isle

8. Explain: We are going to take a much closer look at this community in its own place. We are going to Belfast. Our first contact with the people of this community will be through images and a song which traces a history of the people. Sit or lie down, look and listen. The PowerPoint presentation is shown.

    Normally we would watch it twice; once with the full dramatic impact of the images and song allowed to grow, then with discussion and observation of the images and song invited. What 'characters' have been seen? What is the history of the people traced in the song? How long is their memory? (Nine hundred years). Building upon the reality of the images and the content of the song this should be a focused and serious reflection.

Bridging into character

9. Tell the group: 'In the next part of our work we are going to enter imaginatively into the world of these characters. You have all seen these people now. Remember they are all real people. From your sitting position, I am going to invite you to stand one at a time. As you stand you will be "stepping" into the world of these people and you will speak the people's basic attitude by completing the sentence "My people, a people who..." Prepare this statement. Begin.'

10. Speak to the group: 'We travel to the home community, to Belfast. Think about the people you have seen in the images. Think about their situation. Here is a second song. I am going to sing it to you myself (!) "My Youngest Son Came Home Today". Who are the characters from the song? Mother. Father. Children. Who else might we invent to create a catholic Belfast community; friends, priest, extended family, neighbours?'

Part Three: Whole group drama: the Belfast pub

11. Create a scene in a Belfast pub the night before the dead son's funeral. The pub is at the end of one of the rows of terraces seen earlier. It is a quiet and intimate pub. Allocate the roles. We will now need bar staff as well. (*You* don't yet have a part.) Discuss the use of accents. (Practice your own!)

    Build the set. Mark out the bar: tables, bar, etc.

    Create a whole group tableau. Students enter one at a time and take up the position of their character. As they move into position ask characters to announce themselves: name, relationship to the deceased (we'll call him Michael) and to express their attitude towards him. At this point make it clear that Michael he has been killed, as a member of the IRA, on an operation against the British army. Some people will want revenge, some will not want to lose another member of the community.

    Bring the scene to life. Check for *belief*. Spotlight elements of the scene. Provoke discussion on the central question of revenge or 'settlement'. Work and run the scene. Once the situation and characters are fully established move to the intervention of the teacher-in-role.

    You enter as the IRA local commander. The character must be powerful, still, scathing, dangerous. A plausible accent is effective. You use the information that students have offered during the scene. You demand that those who are crying, stop. This is a time for anger, not tears. You might blame the women for making their men soft. You rant about the British and the 900 years of oppression. You ask for recruits. Who will join you in the struggle? Let the scene develop. Provoke a confrontation. Who here has the strength to take the commander on: the priest; Michael's mother or father or wife or child? An alternative authority seems to always emerge and is a great dramatic nodal point. Leave the group with a challenge: 'Tomorrow members of the IRA will fire a volley of shots over the dead soldier's coffin in the street. This man is a martyr to this community: a hero. I invite those of you here with courage and anger to join us; join the IRA and join the salute.'

This scene has become perhaps the most powerful in the whole of our drama curriculum. At this point in the students' development they have become able to be fully absorbed in dramatic situations. The set up of this scheme with its roots in personal experience, the sense of threat with which we live and the firm ground of reality on which the characters stand is the basis of its effectiveness. The introduction of the teacher-in-role is the point at which the scheme takes flight. It is the most challenging of our teacher-in-role situations but also the most effective and the most rewarding.

The scene will end with people leaving the pub.

Part Four: Around the coffin: small groups

12. This scene is again about building belief. Build a set to represent the coffin. Where possible, use lighting to create a candle-lit, midnight mood; you might even use candles. Explain:

    'The night has ended in conflict and division. We are sending the characters home. In the front room of Michael's house lies the coffin with his cold corpse. In this community bringing the body home before burial is traditional.'

    Remember, at the very start of our work we talked about 'building belief'. This is your responsibility as an actor. Now we come to the major test. How will you build belief in the coffin? How will you enter the room? How will you speak around it? How will you stand in relation to the coffin? How will you speak to it? Around the coffin there will be the sound of quiet prayer and respectful silence. But the events of the pub will continue. Around the coffin, a character will vow to get revenge, to join with the IRA commander in the morning. How will others react? What will they say?

    At this point it will be permissible for students to 'give up' their existing roles from the pub scenes in favour of more 'central' ones – if they so choose. Their aim is to build the situation as plausibly as possible and to explore the pressure of history, family and community on the decisions of the 'committed' individuals. Propose that somewhere in the scene are the seeds of change that have grown in Northern Ireland. Are people simply growing weary of the struggles? Is the IRA moving towards political power? How might this be subtly suggested?

This will be the last scene in our Irish narrative.

Prepare and watch.

Summative discussion

13. Do students/we have a 'cultural memory'? Does history live with us? How did we all know about the bomb? Some of you had stories to tell of your family. Is this a 'cultural memory'? How far back could we go? Why? Why not? Is *our* memory as long? Do we live as if we had no history? Is it significant that in remembering the bombing we only remember a time when *we* were victims? Perhaps victims have the best memories? Perhaps the passions are so strong and the memory so long because these Irish (and other) people understand themselves as victims with wrongs to right.

    Note: Your discussion here will need updating as the situation in Northern Ireland and elsewhere develops.

    Let's think more generally. The issue of the troubles in Ireland has changed a lot since 1996. There is now 'power-sharing', in which both sides in the conflict have come together to form a state. Others still wish to continue the fight...but they are much weaker and smaller in number. The problems are not over but they have changed. Elements of the story of the Manchester bomb have become history in the years since it was first explored with students; but there are new problems; new uses of terror. From what we have looked at and talked about can anybody suggest reasons behind the terrorism of Al Qaeda? Obviously the situation is different and complicated, but there are important things to learn. Think about the reaction of some to George Bush's use of the word 'crusade' in September 2000. What is a crusade? What were 'the crusades'? How long ago were they? Do some people still live with the memory or the results of this after so long? Is this thought right? 'History lives in the minds of the victims of injustice. The victims expect justice and history will not be resolved for them until justice is brought about'? Discuss. Would a 'terrorist' call themselves a 'terrorist'? They might be 'freedom-fighters' or 'holy martyrs'. Who might 'terrorists' call 'terrorists'?

14. Final Moment: Let us see, if after all our discussions, we can summarise our understanding of the 'extreme mind' in a final piece of dramatic insight. Having gained the permission of the group for this final, demanding task, invite them all to find their own space within a wide circle, facing inwards. Propose that we create a simple whole group performance poem that captures, extends and expresses our understanding. You might like to issue

strips of paper for the carefully chosen words to be written and retained. In this final moment, we return to our initial thinking around the word 'terror'. The poem will be called, 'Terror Comes'. This will be our open line and the 'root' for each line of thought. Propose by way of example, 'Terror comes from...', 'Terror comes to...' 'Terror comes and...' etc.

Once the thoughts have been developed and written up privately, they will be gathered together and shared as a whole. You and the group might spend some time ordering the different lines into the most coherent form.

Perform.

Phase 4: Assessment tasks

Following the delivery of a major scheme of work such as this we would ordinarily set a corresponding major assessment task. The assessment is designed to build upon the issues, skills and approaches of the scheme and to embed them in students' practice. Below are two versions of the assessment. The first continues to take the Northern Irish 'Troubles' as its background, the second invites students to explore different historical and cultural settings and to investigate them with the same quality and depth of thought as demonstrated in the scheme. The purpose will be, to understand *something* about the culture of the time/place and to communicate it to the audience.

Each year it becomes necessary to re-write sections of the assessment in order to match the direction and thoughts of the group. Both of these assessments have led to excellent, sometimes profound work.

Research-based drama

Over the past few lessons we have been looking at the world of 'the extremist'; why do people do extreme things? We have looked in particular at terrorist communities in Northern Ireland.

We have seen how history might live powerfully in the people of the community, how nearly every life is touched by 'the Troubles', how people might live with feelings of revenge, guilt, hatred, hope; how a community can be so divided. We have seen how there might be an unending cycle of violence.

In drama terms we have focused on:

1. *Belief* – how do we make an audience believe in our characters and objects, our bombs and our coffins?

2. *Groups* – making groups realistic and dramatic by making all characters **different**, knowing where they fit into the 'pecking order' of the group and creating well-defined conflict between them.
3. *Background* – Setting our drama in a place which is very different from here and now. Learning (and teaching) about the 'other' place.
4. *Atmosphere* – Choosing situations that create atmosphere, tension and meaning.

Assessment task 1: Ireland

Taking what you know of the background to the Troubles in Northern Ireland you are going to research and create your own story. Against this background, which is characterised by anger, history, violence, community and division, you are going to tell the story of a person's struggle for survival, revenge or peace. You might think about it as:

● the child's story
● the soldier's story
● the victim's story
● the mother's story.

The events and situations of the drama should be as emotional, difficult and life-changing as those in the story we have been telling. Great drama places people at the edge of themselves and their situation. Your characters must make a journey through the narrative you build. You should ask yourself:

● How do you allow your audience to engage with and understand your characters?
● What key objects are there in the narrative? How do you build belief in these things? How do you make these things stand for other ideas or things – how do we give them symbolic power? (This might involve how people use the objects, or how they work on stage.)
● In building the drama, what structure will best serve your characters, narrative and your thinking?
● What is the **centre** of your play; a moment, thought, action?

You might like to think about the use of music in your drama and in particular live singing.

Assessment task 2: a time, a place

Create a piece of drama which is set in a particular time or place. You and your group must *research* a specific and distinct time and place. This will involve looking for facts, stories, people, names, poems, songs from the period you choose. You will be given time in the Library and ICT suite. You will also have to do your own research in your own time. Some examples might be: Nazi Germany, South Africa, the Deep South of America in the 1950s, First World War, Hiroshima, Africa in famine, Industrial Revolution in Britain, the Gulf War, etc. In your research you are looking for the human stories that are meaningful to use and build upon.

The events and situations of the drama should be as emotional, difficult and life-changing as those in the story we have been telling. Great drama places people at the edge of themselves and their situation. Your characters must make a *journey* through the narrative you build. You should ask yourself:

● How do you allow your audience to engage and understand your characters?
● What key objects are there in the narrative? How do you build belief in these things? How do you make these things stand for other ideas or things – how do we give them symbolic power? (This might involve how people USE the objects, or how they 'work' on stage).
● In building the drama, what structure will best serve your characters, narrative and your thinking?
● What is the 'centre' of your play; a moment, thought, action?

You might like to think about the use of music in your drama and in particular, live singing.

Year 10/11 scheme: *Tuesday*

Edward Bond's theatre is powerful, sometimes difficult theatre. He creates moments that aim to prise off the lids of the limits that he believes contain us, and invite us to create our own meanings. His plays have provoked outrage and horror, but he is deeply a man of the theatre who understands the needs of his audience. His work, in our experience, has a special power for young people. Over the past number of years he has been writing much for the young. The plays in this series are challenging but rich for children and young people, who can seem to find themselves stumbling into moments of profundity and authenticity. *Tuesday* has a special place in my own teaching experience; the late scene between Irene and the policewoman was the subject of the most electrifying GCSE performance I have been witness to. It still resonates with me after some 12 years. Similarly, other work with young people on Bond's plays (particularly the inter-school residential events that Bond wrote material specifically for) has shown his capacity for communicating so powerfully with young people in ways that continue to surprise. He seems to have routes into the contemporary mind that are unique and compelling.

In the scheme that follows, we take a look at a play that was written for the BBC's School Programme – though subsequently performed on the stage. In it, a teenage girl is studying for her exams under the watchful eye of her controlling father. Suddenly, her boyfriend Brian, a young soldier, returns from active service seeking refuge. The Methuen publication of the book (the version in which it appears on its own) includes some useful classroom-orientated notes, including interviews with the actors who appeared in the first BBC production and additional material from Edward Bond.

The scheme will end with practical assessments of sections of the play performed by students. We are, therefore, using this sequence of exploratory drama techniques as an extended rehearsal process which aims to give our young actors access to the play and characters in a detailed and practical way. Our expectation will be that the resulting scripted performances will be rich and compelling, built as they will be, on understanding and empathy.

Phase 1: Analysing the situation

Part One: The room and the gun

In this first phase we take students to the narrative centre of the play (though not, perhaps, the aesthetic centre). We find ourselves in a compelling situation; a teenager's bedroom, a parent, a uniformed outsider and a gun. At this moment in the text, the problem and meaning of the situation is yet to be explored, but here we set students in the centre of the situation and invite them to fill the gap.

1. Mark out a square the size of a small bedroom on the floor (or a series of such squares – one for each group). Form groups of three. Explain that there are three people in this room – parent, child and another *not* from the immediate family but known well to the other two – we shall call them 'the other'. Now explain that there is also, in this small room, a gun: you might choose to have a simple object to signify the gun – something made simply from paper compacted with masking tape to form the shape, perhaps. You might of course, prefer to use an object of more weight and reality – a die-cast toy gun or similar perhaps.

2. Using one of the groups as markers of the situation, establish the following tableau – without indicating *which character is which*.

   Character 1 is standing calmly, watching the event.
   Character 2 is on the floor begging and shielding him/herself.
   Character 3 has the gun held outstretched, pointed at Character 2.

   There are three key problems for the groups:

   i. Of the three *available* characters – child, parent, 'other' – who in this situation is who? Clearly, there are several permutations. The groups should discuss and explore the different options before settling on one. What options might surprise us? Such a surprise might make us reconsider our assumptions . . . the things we think we understand. This is a useful and important thing to do in drama.
   ii. Once you have settled upon a situation, you will need to make sense of it for yourselves, that is, to be clear in your own minds how this situation could have come about. What steps might have brought these three people to this moment? What is each character's situation and motivation – and what is their relationship with the other two characters?

iii. How will you communicate the necessary information to your audience? What do the audience need to know to understand this situation? Of course, they will need to know who is who . . . perhaps a simple thing, but also consider this: how will you 'load' the necessary information into the few moments of drama you will show, in as efficient a way as possible, in as few words, with as little action? Such 'loading' and 'focusing' of the drama is a high-order skill.

The students' task will be to imagine the centre of the play. It doesn't matter for the moment what Edward Bond's situation is, this is a chance for them to fill the gap with their own imaginative responses to the outlined situation. There is possibly an element of 'soap opera' about the situation, but our insistence on clarity and our later exploration of the aesthetic centre take us somewhere deeper: as ever, the drama isn't about the action itself, but the *meaning* of the action.

Give groups time to develop and hone their dramas.

When it comes to performance, watch the dramas in an 'active' way. What signs does each drama give the audience to allow them to understand the situation? How do the audience read these signs and what do they understand from them? Or rather, what meanings do the audience create from the signs that are given?

3. At the end of the discussion, step back from the different narratives on offer. Explain that this is a situation from the heart of a short play written for young people by one of our most important and serious playwrights. You might like to explore Bond's history and impact further – there is a page of images and resources available on our own website as listed below in the bibliography.

If such an important playwright – a man of 'big ideas' – has created this situation, you might expect that he has in mind his own 'big idea' – he is giving his own signs to point to something he would like us to think about. It probably won't be a simple moral – 'Be good to your children' – it will be inviting (perhaps forcing) us to look at and think about a particular area of life. In which case, from what you know right now . . . before we look at his story . . . what area of life do you think he wants us to look at? What is he interested in here?

Allow this discussion to develop. The suggestions made will be reflective of the situations that the students have created themselves. You might find you are marking out territory that students themselves wish to consider – which might, or might not, correspond with Bond's areas of interest.

Part Two: Enacting the story: a 'whoosh!'

4.   Ask if students are sufficiently interested to want to know more about Bond's play (of course they are). Now, propose that you could read the text or find a copy of the original television play to watch, but perhaps the group should try to make its own exploration of the play, called simply *Tuesday*, something more dynamic; something that has reality on the stage. Propose the 'story whoosh!' technique and explain its processes (if you need to). This will be a serious-minded kind of 'whooshing!', but, as always it will be useful to enact the broad sweep of the narrative before we come to look at the details, so that the context of the detail is understood.

5.   So, gather the group into a large circle around one of the marked out bedroom squares. As a preliminary task, you might give the names of the characters; Irene, Brian and Father. What might these names suggest? They will have been carefully picked. You might like to add a table and chair, a bed, a window and a door. This is a fairly simple, but long narrative. It is in three parts and you might like to deal with each part on its own . . . or pause briefly between each one.

   Here are the stages in the narrative of *Tuesday*.

Part 1

● A teenage girl, Irene, is studying for her exams. The room is clear and tidy.
● There is a knock on the door below. Again. Irene goes to answer it. Brian, Irene's boyfriend, enters the bedroom. He is agitated. He is a soldier and should be at war. He has come to Irene to ask her to hide him. He places a pistol under Irene's pillow without her seeing.
● Irene tries to encourage Brian to tell her why he has run away. He can't. He says he won't go back. But something has happened which he can't talk about . . .
● Father returns below. 'Home!' Brian asks Irene not to tell him. He tries to hide under her small, low bed. She says, 'It's his house,' and goes down.

Whoosh! (Simply change actors)

● Father enters. He speaks calmly; as if he would help Brian and find a solution. He makes inappropriate jokes that aren't funny.
● The young soldier Brian won't say why he is here or why he has deserted.

- Irene comes to the door. Father orders her back downstairs. She goes. Father tries to take control and send Brian back to barracks. Brian calls for Irene to come. Father tells her to stay down. Brian says he will leave. Father blocks his way at the door. Irene comes in and goes to Brian.

- Father shares a story about his own wartime experience; dead soldiers with legs sticking out of a tank. He assumes it is because of the terrible things Brian has seen on the battlefield that he has left the army. It isn't. Father becomes very angry. Brian takes out the gun.

- Brian makes father go down on his knees and then dance like the dying soldiers in the tank... Irene watches. She then takes the gun from Brian and tells Father to get up.

- Father then begins to humiliate Brian because he gave his gun away to 'a girl'. Irene says she'll run away with Brian. Father turns on her – calling her a 'Pathetic little tart!' He rants and humiliates them both. Irene raises the gun and points it at her father.

- She pulls the trigger. Nothing. She aims carefully and pulls it again. Her hands shake. She steadies them and pulls the trigger. Nothing. The gun is empty.

- Brian takes the gun. Father is now terrified of Irene, as she moves past him he screams: 'She's got a knife' – she hasn't. He wants to know, 'Did she know it was not loaded? Did she know?' Irene says: "Sometimes there is a terrible tragedy. You have to play your part."

Whoosh! (Simply change actors again.) (You might break here for brief questions or to check responses.)

Part 2

- Brian and Father are staring at Irene, who is staring at the exam papers. Father is still reeling from Irene's action. 'I can't live with her here. This house isn't mine anymore.' He goes downstairs saying he needs to be sick.

- Brian says he will hand himself in. He asks Irene why she did it. He saw the killer's look in her eyes. He tells her why he really deserted. A simple event in the desert that Brian reads as a revelation...

- One day, off duty, Brian went for a walk in the desert. He saw a child coming towards him over a dune. He tried to stop the child but the child simply walked away into the desert. Brian tried to follow... but the sand seemed turned to mud to stop him. The child walked away.

- Brian says, 'The sand was opening up between us. A child is lifted from its mother – the chord stretches. It walked away, from its father – mother – us. Children are meant to cry for food. For cold. The dark. Alone. For comfort. It walked away. From everyone. We hate and kill. It had had enough. Children have begun to walk away from human beings . . . I can't forget the child. I went for the wrong walk. I met myself.'

- This is why he left the army; not a terrible, bloody incident – though there were many of those – but because of a simple incident that illuminated Brian's understanding of himself and the world; a *vision*. He came to Irene because he thought that she would understand. But now he rejects her.

Whoosh!

- Father returns to the room. His behaviour is different. He has taken off his shoes. He has called the police and been told to try and keep Brian in the room until they arrive. Though he stupidly won't admit this.

- To give him *something* Brian tells Father the gruesome, violent story of an enemy soldier being bayoneted to death as he screams for his mother. Father is happy now: **'So what was all the fuss for!'** Irene looks through the window and says the police have arrived: road-blocks, on the roof, helicopters swarming. Irene says Father must have told them he had a gun.

- An officer leans into the room and orders Brian to drop the gun. 'No . . .' A shot. Brian is hit. He puts his hand into his jacket and takes it out covered in blood. He says, 'Let me live. Let me live.' He slips down the wall leaving a bloody mark.

- An army of police officers – including a dog – come through the windows and door and surround Brian with guns. Radios, megaphones and a helicopter fill the air. A deafening commotion; authority invades Irene's bedroom. Paramedics attend to Brian, putting a mask over his face.

- A neighbour enters with a small child. She accidentally kicks the gun which goes to Brian's hand. He picks it up and holds it out. Silence. Everyone watches. The gun falls. An officer jumps on Brian's chest. Only the child sees that he was trying to hand it over. The neighbour is ordered out and people begin to leave.

- Irene has her hands flat on her desk. She is shaking like a clairvoyant. Trembling.

Part 3

- A few police and medics are still hanging about. Brian lies covered in a sheet. The police are talking and justifying the shooting. Father is doing the same.

- Father goes to talk to Irene saying, 'It won't be easy to get back to normal tomorrow.' He tries to explain and make light of her trying to kill him. Irene keeps repeating, 'I thought the gun had bullets in it. I tried to kill you.' He wants her to play along with his pretence that it didn't happen; to apologise.

- When she does, he won't believe her.

- Brian is taken away. He dies in the hallway downstairs.

- Father struggles to pull a tiny button off his shirt . . . one that Irene sewed on for him. He won't have it anymore. Irene says, 'I tried to kill you. It was right.' He says she needs help; he is broken and desperate and terrified. He begs her to stop. He promises that things will be different in the future. 'In a way you've set me free. There's nothing to pretend.' Everyone has now gone.

- Father stands in the chalk mark showing where Brian had fallen. He draws another chalk mark around his own feet. Irene says, 'I can't tell you why I did it. I don't know the words. No one taught them to me.' Father says he's glad Brian is dead and exits.

- Irene wraps herself in a grey blanket and sits on the bed. She looks like an old woman. A policewoman arrives; incredibly smart and in control. Irene speaks about trying to kill her father and how the moment has given her clarity. '. . . there was a child . . . it walked . . . away . . .'. The officer offers some inane and foolish sympathy. Irene says to her 'Poor woman'. Irene hands her a bottle of her make-up. The officer seems childishly pleased.

- Irene lies down to sleep. 'She is young again.' The officer stands guard by the window. As she falls into sleep, Irene repeats: 'Let me live. Let me live.'

Whoosh!

The End.

6. Following the enactment, discuss the story. What questions do the group have? There may be questions about the characters and their motivations, key actions, events, etc. You might have questions of your own. Why did

Brian leave the army? Why are there so many police officers in the room? Why does Father pull a single button off? Why does Irene try to shoot her father? Why does Brian reject Irene? Why do the police shoot Brian? Why the play is called *Tuesday*?

Explain that we are now going to look in more detail at certain aspects of the play which might touch upon some of the ideas we've begun to think about in our discussion.

Part Three: Exploring Brian's character

The soldier

7.   Brian has deserted from the army – 'gone AWOL' (absent without leave). That is a serious military crime. Why did he leave? Father assumes – perhaps because he has some kind of military background himself – that it is the 'horror' of war that has driven him away. Brian has seen terrible things – he tells of the bayoneting incident – but there is also the issue of the child in the desert. In this part, we are going to look at the two speeches that give an account of both incidents: the horror and the vision.

We are going to look in detail at the speeches through a simple process of breaking down, 'interrogating' and performing each one in turn. The first is more graphic and straightforward but the second presents us with much more interesting and creative problems of performance and meaning. Although the two speeches are written for a single character – Brian – we will be looking at them and performing them as a group. You might like to think of the process as one of a 'group mind'. We will extend this notion when we come to look at Brian's character at the end of the second speech.

The horror

8.   There are two visions of horror in the play – Father's and Brian's. We are going to look at the text of Brian's account. We have divided the speech into six parts (see Resource 1 below). Distribute these to six groups and invite them to read, discuss and prepare to perform the text. In this first instance, we propose trying to simply read the speech but as a kind of relay race. Not only will the six groups hand over from one to the next, but each group will also sub-divide their portion into small units of text and distribute these amongst themselves. In this way, we might even attempt a learnt performance of the speech. Once the sub-division and learning has been

accomplished, call the group together into a circle in the order in which the lines are spoken. Explain the following:

You are all Brian. This is a rehearsal for the delivery of Brian's speech. When we speak we will need to work together as if we were **one actor**. Firstly, let us hear all of the lines one after the other. You can speak the lines in a simple fashion. (Demonstrate this by reading a few lines yourself.)

So how should this speech be delivered? Who is he talking to; in what circumstances? Is it a highly significant speech to Brian? Or is he trying to humour Father... or get him 'off his back'? How does this change how it might be spoken? Let's try it again with this sense.

You might try the speech several times in a variety of ways:

● as a bragging soldier – at some pace
● as a storyteller trying to captivate an audience
● as someone trying to scare the listener.

Each time, ask the group to take up the physical stance of the soldier as he speaks; this will effect how the lines are spoken. Discuss the effects and impact of the different versions.

What is this speech for? What does it accomplish? What does it capture? What do you notice about it? What surprises you? What questions do you have about the speech; about Brian?

The centre

9. Invite each group to find the 'centre', or 'central image' of the section they have been given, and to prepare to perform this as an illustration of the text. Explain that a central image is a tableau that summarises, or gets to the heart of the meaning or action of the text. It might usefully involve a simple gesture or movement. The groups will then prepare and perform these 'gestural centres' alongside the text – in a continuous performance around the space.

10. In discussion with the group pull out some key elements of the violent scene described. Does the scene have an impact on Brian and those who hear it in the room? Has such war-time butchery become ordinary to him... perhaps like Father's tank story? Has he become desensitised to it? Have we? Why does he tell this story to Father? Is he being kind by giving him something that he will readily understand? Or is he making a fool of him?

So, if it is not the so-called 'Horrors of War' that makes him desert the army, what is it; the sight of a walking child? Does anybody understand this? Is it a 'vision'? Does Brian experience it as one? What is the power of a vision? Could we say that Brian 'makes meaning' out of this simple event? Should we have a look at it in this second speech?

The vision

11. For this section, we shall be looking at Brian's long speech about the child in the desert. We again offer a simple breakdown of the speech into manageable chunks or 'units' (Resource 2 below). To begin the process, you might read it yourself in its entirety before distributing the units as for the previous speech. Again, work towards the 'centre' of the speech/ incident but now try to capture this in the simple spoken delivery of the speech. We suggest that you do NOT now enact the gestural centre of each unit as earlier, but instead, think precisely about the delivery of each line and load the spoken text with meaning. The soldier is still. The text will do the work. Perhaps he sees the vision before him again.

Work towards a continuous round-the-circle performance of the whole speech; stopping in the early stages to give students the chance to notice what they will about the speech and discuss these ideas. Encourage them to be as alert as possible to the sense, the impact, the effects of the speech. When it is felt that the group has gleaned as much as they can from the speech, propose a final performance which is to be captured as a permanent record of the group's work in the form of a simple audio recording. Audio recordings can be useful in focusing on the expression of the text and are also less intrusive and inhibiting than video recording. Copies of the recording can also be easily distributed to the group for further study or simple interest.

Questions that might arise – or you might provoke: Who is he telling the story to? Why; in what circumstances? What has happened just before? Does Irene understand the story? She refers to it later. What is the story about? To answer this, we might reflect upon the simple actions of the incident, but there is also the meaning of the incident. How do the two characters (Brian and the child) relate to the desert environment? Who is more at home in the desert? What does Brian understand; that children have begun to reject the adult world? What does this mean? Is it true? Is it a new phenomenon? Why might a child reject an adult's vision of the world? Does Irene do something similar to her father? Is turning the gun on her father like walking away? How can such visions change a person's life? What do you think is the writer's vision of the world? What line is the centre of the speech?

Brian – A distributed hot-seat

12. Reflect upon the impact of the story of the child on Brian. Could he explain it? What would he have to say if we were to stop and question him immediately after he had given the speech? Does the group think that it could speak for him? In preparation for the following, gather together everything that we know about Brian. You might write these down on scraps of paper and stick them to a human outline on a wall or around a central object representing the soldier (Khaki clothes, a helmet, some boots perhaps). Once all scraps of information about the character have been gathered, bridge into the 'distributed hot-seat' by reading them all out formally, perhaps using a sentence root such as 'Brian, the soldier who…'

13. Now send the group to sit on chairs facing away from others and to take up the stance of Brian at the end of the speech. They are ALL Brian. You will question them and anyone can answer by simply looking at you or indicating with a gesture that they are prepared to answer your questions. You might usefully adopt a gently hostile, interrogative tone of voice; you want to understand this wayward young lad…but are growing impatient.

    Questions you might ask: Why have you come to Irene's house; to her bedroom? What has she done to change how you feel about her? What do you think about her father? Did you used to enjoy army life? What has changed? What happened in the desert? Are you a coward? Why are you telling Irene this story? What did you think she could do to help you? Can she still help you? Why? Why not? Why did you bring a gun? Of course, as the replies come, follow these new lines of thinking and respond to further replies. The effect of the distributed character is hopefully to build a rich and diverse sense of his complexity and depth.

    Once the hot-seat activity is complete ask the group to come out of role to reflect upon Brian. How do they understand him now? How might this understanding have changed? What does he want? Is he a character they *like* or sympathise with?

Part Four: Exploring authority and power balance

The parent and child

14. It might be useful to think of the play as one about **authority**. What authorities are there in the play? Father, Army, Police, school (in the form of exams?). What does the play ask about authority? Irene is 'a good girl'; how do we know this? What evidence is there of the father's control over her? The changes in power in the play between the two characters might be thought of as a pendulum swinging between the two or as a kind of 'dance' in which the person leading the dance – having control – changes from moment to moment.

A dance of power

15. Ask the group to consider how you might show the differences in power between two people in a tableau with movement. You can demonstrate this very simply with a volunteer: the tableau being clear and strong and the movement being slow and expressive of force and changing force. Now add a line of text to complete your modelling; a line which pinpoints the 'nodal' point of the relationship as the balance of power shifts. Michael Rosen uses the term 'the elbow of the narrative' to describe such shifts in direction and power. For example, Father's line, 'I can't live with her here. This house isn't mine anymore.' Propose that in pairs the students look very closely at the father–daughter relationship and track the changes throughout the play by creating 'tableau-and-text' sequences. You might find it useful to split the group into three and allocate each of the three parts of the play accordingly.

    This is an exercise which will force students to look very closely at the text, sub-text and 'meta-text'. 'Meta-text' is a term used by Bond to point us in the direction not of the hidden, private or perhaps psychological meaning of moments of drama (the familiar 'sub-text'), but to the over-arching points of reference in philosophy, history, sociology, politics, etc. With a sense of relish, he looks for and leads us to both 'the kitchen table and the edge of the universe', in the same moment.

    This is quite a demanding task and you might consider breaking it down even further, for example, by asking pairs to look for just one such nodal moment in a given selection of text.

    Once the identifications of text and moments and the representations of these are complete, perform them all as a continuous sequence. Music might add to the sense of theatre of this moment.

An encounter

16. Now that we have looked closely at the relationship between these two central characters we shall move on to produce an encounter between the two. Our improvisation of the characters must tie itself tightly to the information offered by Bond's text. We can't contradict the carefully-constructed details, but we can 'build-out' from them and allow ourselves to try and inhabit their situations.

    Recount that in a famous play called *The Caucasian Chalk Circle* Bertholt Brecht uses a powerful form of words to uncover a character's inner thought processes by saying, 'Listen to what she thought, but did not say...'. We have mentioned this in earlier schemes. It seems to be a simple truth that people do not always SAY exactly what they might WANT to say. There are many reasons why we are not always completely truthful – many of them perfectly good reasons. But what if we could make our characters speak their hidden thoughts... and address them to each other? In the play Irene says, 'I don't know why I did it. I don't know the words. Nobody taught them to me.' Perhaps here, we can give Irene the words she needs.

17. Explain that we are going to set up a simple situation – similar to the Brian 'distributed hot-seat' – but in which the two characters are going to speak to each other in all honesty – for once. The students are already in role from the previous exercise, now ask the group to split into two and send all those playing Irene to one side of the room facing inwards and all the Fathers to the other side facing across the space towards the Irene group. Explain that again, we are going to distribute the characters' *mind* across the group; anyone can answer the questions you pose. It is an 'encounter' in the sense that it is a frank exchange of thoughts outside of the naturalistic setting of the play; it has the sense of something like a family counselling session with you loosely in role as the facilitator of the session. Underline that the characters must stay within the world of the play; you will not be asking questions that are too speculative or beyond the narrative facts (for example, about Irene's mother) but ones that deepen our understanding of the situation and characters of the play itself. It might be necessary to indicate just where on the timeline of the play our encounter occurs. We would propose a moment after the gun incident but before the shooting of Brian. This will allow you to deal with heart of the drama before its resolution.

    Note: an alternative to the process described above is to have the pairs work together again – to seat them in front of each other but still to respond to your questions. The advantage of the *group* version is that the thinking is shared and accumulates to develop greater depth and insight. You might develop your own process which might integrate the pair and group approaches.

The approach of your questioning will be to probe and press. The key areas of understanding to explore – built out by implication from the text – are perhaps:

- Their relationship before Brian's arrival: what was Irene's role in the house? How was Father's authority expressed?
- The impact of Brian's arrival: how did each of them respond to him? How do they feel about him ordinarily? What do they think is Brian's issue with the army?
- Irene's aiming of the gun at her father: at which moment did she decide to do this? How did Father feel at this moment? Can he understand why she did it? Can Irene understand her own action?
- More generally: How would they describe their life together? Does Father feel that he controls his daughter? Does Irene feel controlled? What do they wish they could say to each other? What do they wish they could change in their lives together?

At the end of the sequence bring the students out of their roles and ask them to reflect upon what they have understood about the two characters. Remind the group that Bond's characters don't only have reality as 'people' – in a naturalistic sense – but importantly, as characters who represent and embody critical thinking about the world; they are 'meta-textual' creations. What do you think the characters – parent and child – represent or lead us to think about? Bond's characters have a 'use'. Bond is encouraging reaction and thought – what is their 'use'?

18. To finish this section, invite the group to adopt their characters one last time. Invite the group to walk to a new spot in the space and to melt into a tableau of their character at the very END of the play. Give each character an indicative line of where their journey ends in the play: Father: 'If I kill myself tomorrow, would you be sorry?' and Irene: 'What day is it? I must lie down now. Sleep. Now. Tomorrow... Let me live. Let me live.' Bring the group into the stillness of this final set of images. Give the group the opportunity to complete the moment by giving their own spoken text to their character as a final statement of their journey.

Extending activity

There are two other elements of the play which might offer an interesting additional exploration and possibly a break in style from the other areas of work.

- *The button* – In Part 3, Father gives his attention to a button on a shirt – one that Irene sewed on for him. (What might this tell you about their relationship?) It is an interesting moment in which perhaps the smallest and most insignificant object (a button) is given immense meaning and significance; for the Father at that time, it represents their old relationship and perhaps Irene's domestic care of him. This theatrical imbuing of an object with super-meaning is what Bond calls 'cathexis'; it's a button . . . but at that moment it's as if it is his whole universe – that he would tear off and stuff down his daughter's throat. As an acting exercise ask the group to consider just how he might try to pull the button off to imbue the action with 'super-meaning'.
- *The police* When the police arrive, they arrive like a terrifying, noisy swarm. Read the description and get a sense of the sudden entrance and the impact it has on this simple play about three people in a bedroom. Mark a small square on the floor and play a game – like Sardines – in which everybody in the class must squeeze into the small room-shape. They must enter suddenly, noisily, dangerously, with calls that summon the idea of the armed police entering. (Where have the police been waiting? Just beyond the walls?) You might add a helicopter sound effect. The simple, physical game might involve an 'in' and 'out' situation. 'Out' involves the group quietly and calmly walking around the room waiting for your call. On a call of 'Go! Go! Go!' the group must all immediately rush noisily into the space and maintain the sense of 'invasion' until you give the call for them to move back out of the space with 'Nothing to see here . . . Nothing to see . . .'. After the 'game' discuss this element of the play; why does Bond so strikingly fill the stage with a waiting police force? What is the meaning of this?

Phase 2: Into scripted performance

At the end of this extended sequence of activities, the group is ready to begin its own scripted performance of the play. The play breaks down into easily identifiable 'units' of drama and small groups should be encouraged to focus in on specific units that meet their interests, strengths and needs as performers. You might consider it useful to have each of the groups perform different units of the play such that you could assemble a full performance of the whole play by simply linking them together. With the exploration that the scheme has offered, we would hope that students are able to easily access the script and give a well-developed theatrical realisation of it.

Resource 1:
Brian's speech on the killing of an enemy prisoner

1. Listen. There was a hill. They're dug in on the top. We came up fighting. Mortars. Grenades. Went in. Cleared it out. We were in a space. Like a room – so flat you could've laid a carpet – rocks sticking up like bits left of the walls. Their dead on the floor. Their wounded shivering on the rocks.

2. Quiet. The wounded snivelling – the odd sounds of fighting – made it quieter. Fags out, lit up. Ping on the rock. We've got a sniper. Then one of theirs – wound in the gut – started to whine for mum. Same word in any language. It gets louder.

3. One of ours – nerves gone – goes over to theirs yelling shut it, shut it – tries sign language with the bayonet. Theirs: mmeeoowwm-muummhhaa – like a soccer chant. Ours screaming: not words now – warning – orders – reasons – praying – telling how'd-I-know? – a bedtime story to make him stop

4. – on and on – my language – the language I dream in – this language – but I don't know it – screaming – an animal down his throat he's sicking up, it's digging down. Theirs: maawah – maawah – maawah! Ours: screaming. Theirs: maawah – staring in God's face screaming with a bayonet on judgement day.

5. ...ping that's the sniper – and God screams and puts the bayonet in – in the wounded belly – in the wha-wha – and their arms go up as if it wants to embrace – then fall back to its sides – and flap – like wings on a dead bird falling in the sky

6. – and ours stops jabbing – theirs: a bit of blood pops from its mouth and dribbles down its chin – ours mutters as he wipes his bayonet on their jacket. God smokes. The fag still in his mouth. Didn't go out. I didn't understand my language.

Resource 2:
The child in the desert speech

(Note: the breaks in the text are our own)

1. Everyone's in a room like this. I don't know how we live in it. I'll tell you.
    I want to know if you can still understand. It's not much of a story. It was
    in the desert. A temporary hold-up. A few days quiet before the order
    to go in. Even in war you can slip away. I took a walk in no-man's land.

2. The dunes. Covered in long neat rows of little waves. Beautiful. Then,
    where they were slashed open by tanks. Machines dragging their
    graves behind them. I passed there and went on. It was still. Flat. Sand.
    Flatter than the sky. I saw – how far? – a shadow. Black. Dot. A
    periscope sticking up from a secret dug-out? No, it was a moving
    shadow.

3. First I didn't see the thing that made it. Lost in the heat. Then I saw
    something white. Walking on the shadow. A mirage? In war you're in
    the mirage. I got closer. A man. A dwarf. Walking on its own shadow. I
    should've turned back. Against orders being there. You must see
    everything. It's not given to you again. A little chap walking away. The
    shadow round his feet. Five? Six? It wore a white thing.

4. I thought I was silent in the sand. Sand must make many sounds. He
    knew them all. It was a different place for him. He turned and looked
    straight over his shoulder. *At* me. No expression – but he saw. I couldn't
    shout. I was afraid the sand would hear me and try to bury me. I
    pointed my gun. What else could I do? Not in anger. It was a pointed
    finger made of metal.

5. He looked over his shoulder and went on. Didn't hurry. His face didn't
    change. I don't know if he was calm. I ran. Fell. The sand was ice to me.
    I slid – digging in – trying to get to my feet. In my eyes and mouth and
    colour. That was worse. It trickled down my back as if, as if . . . I
    shuddered. I reached him. He went on. Didn't flinch or change his line.
    The sand didn't hurt him – I tore it to bits just being there.

6. I stumbled beside him. Put out my hand. I couldn't touch him. Speak
    English? Speeky lingleesh? I was crying. Spitting sand. Tell me, tell me,
    tell me . . . He didn't answer. He didn't have the words. He went on.

7. Sometimes now I speak – ordinary things. Shut the door – more tea –
    and there's bits of sand in my mouth. I fell back. Let him go. I was lost.
    Crying. The sand was turning to scum – mud –on my face. He didn't

look around. Went on. He knew I couldn't hurt him. Some of our planes rose up on the horizon and went down again. The sand was opening up between us.

8. A child is lifted from its mother – the chord stretches. It walked away, from its father – mother – us. Children are meant to cry for food. For cold. The dark. Alone. For comfort. It walked away. From everyone. We hate and kill. It had had enough. Children have begun to walk away from human beings...

9. I let it go – to grow up into one of theirs to kill us. I went back to my unit. Slow – the desert was a lump of mud stuck to my boots. We got the order. Went to war. Killed. Then home. Bands. Streamers. Celebrations. I can't forget the child. I went for the wrong walk. I met myself.

The End.

Year 11 scheme: *Faces*

In this simply-structured scheme of work students are led into the creation of a character in some depth. Following the teacher-led input students are invited to take their characters into their own worlds and tell the story of their interactions.

The scheme has become, customarily, the final piece of drama created at the end of the two-year GCSE course. It is a definite act of 'jump off' in which students are invited to become fully absorbed in characterisation and to take full and final responsibility for creating the narrative.

The scheme revolves around a set of portrait paintings by the American photo-realist painter Chuck Brown. Over time these have been augmented with portraits gleaned from internet searches. The characters are set up as struggling, imperfect, realistic individuals. To use Edward Bond's useful form of words, they are not 'at home in the world'. Students are invited to explore their characters' limitations and the reasons for them. As far as possible, students are offered a free rein to respond instinctively and with imagination; the questioning that lies in the early stages of the scheme and which provokes the initial thinking and creative decision-making, should be fully open.

Phase 1: Building a character

Part One: Ritual opening

1. Before the students' entry, set out chairs such that a person sitting in them would not be looking directly at another person. In another space lay down the pictures of the faces, face-down in two areas, male and female. Lighting and sound, where available, should be used to ritualise the space. The use of spoken word recordings is recommended. These should be played at a level at which the words are barely audible. In the past, recordings of Dylan Thomas reading his own work have been very effective because of the

'attack' in the delivery. Self-help programmes have also been effective. The sound content here is an important part of the texture of the opening. The presence of the spoken word in the working space gives a sense of entering another's world, thick with private thinking.

2.   Students enter one at a time. They are asked to go to the faces and choose one. They take it to a seat and sit in silence looking at the face; searching for information about the person and building an imaginative sense of just who they are. This continues until the whole group is assembled. Of course, it is important to insist on silence and stillness. The vocal background track fills the silence with the impression of insistent, inescapable thought.

Part Two: Unfolding the character: building an emotional content

3.   You begin, slowly and thoughtfully:

> *There is no perfect human face. Look at this face. <u>This</u> is going to be your face. It isn't perfect. Sometimes you hate it. What does this character hate about their face? Look at it closely. WAIT. We are going to begin the process of creating a character. This character, this **person** who doesn't yet exist, and won't do so until they are created by you – this person you are going to take on a journey. You are going to invent their past life, explore their current situation and send them off into the future. These people will give us the stories we will tell in what may be the last piece of drama we ever make together… Look into the face.*
>
> *When this person thinks about their life and the world, how do they feel? What simple word sums up their feeling? Broken? Lost? Alone? Hurt? Decide on this word. Mouth the words to yourself. Use your mouth but do not let anyone else hear.*

4.   Continue:

> *Look at the face. Hold it in front of your own. Now imagine you are holding a mirror. Look into it. Looking back at you is your own face. Hold the sheet in one hand. With the other hand touch your face. Try to imagine that what you are touching is what you can see in the picture. WAIT. Where is the mirror you are looking at? Bathroom? Bedroom? Hall? A hand mirror? A reflection in a shop or train window? WAIT. As you look at yourself you might speak to yourself. What might you say*

about your face? Again, you are going to mouth these words without anyone hearing them. You'll notice, even without making a full sound that your voice is different, it is made differently in your throat and mouth. Notice this as you speak.

5. Pose the following very quickly.

    Answer these questions: Who do you love most? Who do you live with? What colour is your front door? Where is home? Are you at home there? Who do you fear? Where is the safest place you know? WAIT.

    Let students answer the questions with mouthing.

Building the physical

6. *We are going to send you out into the world. How do you feel about that? Actors often say that the most important thing to discover about the character they are playing is their 'physicality', meaning their bodies and their movements. We all have the body that has been given to us by the life we live; the job we do, the food we eat, the way we feel about being in the world. We are now going to find the body of the person who has this face. How does this person sit on a chair? Think this through and shift on your chair until it feels right. Wait. Now. How does this person walk? How does this person touch the floor as they walk? Heavily? Lightly? How does this person move in the world of other people? How do they react when they are around other people? WAIT. I am going to ask you, one at a time, to stand and travel around the room. You must not look at another person. When you start walking you may find yourself walking as yourself and it may take some time for you to 'walk into' the character. That's OK. As you walk you will be discovering your character's 'body'. You may change your speed, posture, eye contact pattern. When you think you've found the character's walk you can sit down in another chair. We are about to begin. When I touch you on the shoulder you may begin your walk. Begin this sequence.*

Environment and action in context.

7. *Our people are alone in their rooms. For a moment paint a picture in your mind of your character's room. This room is their place of safety. It is where they retreat from the world. In the room there are a number of*

*things which make them feel able to rest. Some things that they have accumulated during their lives. As you sit in the room now look around and mouth the names of five things that you can see. As you do so move your head to look in the direction of the object. What are you doing right now in this room? Do it. Concentrate on just this one thing. Live through the **doing** of these actions.*

8.   *We are going to send you out again into the world, but this time to interact with other people. How do you feel about this? What preparations do you have to make? Are you going to shave? Wash? Put make-up on? Brush your hair? Etc. Decide what preparations are necessary. In a moment you are going to perform these actions. As they prepare each of the characters will speak to themselves. Now you will be doing more than simple mouthing. Now you must speak. Perhaps even so quietly that no-one can hear what you are saying, but you should feel yourself into the character's voice. Just as you have felt yourself into their movement. How do they speak? How is it different from your own speech? Accent? Speed? Tone? Using a different part of your throat or mouth? It should FEEL different to speak as this person...just as it should feel different to walk like them. Prepare to begin your preparations for going out. You are free to move around within the limits of your room but nowhere else. Begin.*

Leave students to become absorbed in these detailed private preparations.

Preparation for interaction

9.   *Your character feels uncomfortable around other people. But they are going out...they are going to a self-help group for people, like your character, who struggle to feel at home in the world. People who feel vulnerable. At this meeting you will meet the other characters and I will be in role. Think about the journey you are now going to make. I am going to take a chair and begin a circle. When you are ready you are going to take a chair and join me in the circle. Now stand. Walk to your door. Turn around and look into your room. Turn off the light. Leave.*

10. Around this point an hour-long lesson would probably be coming to a close. Tell students to think about their characters and set a piece of 'actor's research' to see if they can find anybody in the real world who reminds them of the character. Just as they go about their lives, be observant of other people. Tell students that in the next lesson the characters must have

a story to tell about themselves. They should prepare the outline of this story; the story has made them who they are today.

This has been a long and slow lesson. In our own experience it has never failed to generate the appropriate response. Students respond to the serious nature of the undertaking and to the struggling nature of their creations. They also respond to the responsibility handed to them in the creation of their characters and, when the scheme is placed at the terminal point of the course, they respond to the challenge of creating their finest, final drama.

In the first section of the second phase we will slow the process of creation down even further before we begin to present our characters in a dramatic situation. The creation of the written 'monologue map' is an essential aid for less confident actors who are about to be faced with probably their biggest performance challenge to date: an original, extended monologue in an atmosphere of full seriousness.

Phase 2: Telling the character's story

Part One: Preparing to share

11. Lay the chairs out as at the start of the last lesson. Put the face images on the chairs. Play the spoken word track. Students enter in ritual fashion as established earlier. This time they have to find their picture and sit with it. On each chair there will also be paper, a pencil and perhaps a clipboard to lean on.
12. You begin:

    I expect you all to have thought through your character; to have imagined more of a life for them. Very soon we will be taking this set of characters into the group situation described last session. Now take up the picture. Look at the face. Remind yourself of who you are going to be. Look closely. Now pick up the pencil and prepare to write. Think about the story you have imagined for your character. Now write down the following, not in a list but across the page in the style of a simple spider-diagram spreading out from a central circled character-name.

    You might like to show an example of your proposed layout. (See Figure 1)
    Now begin, write:
    Your name.

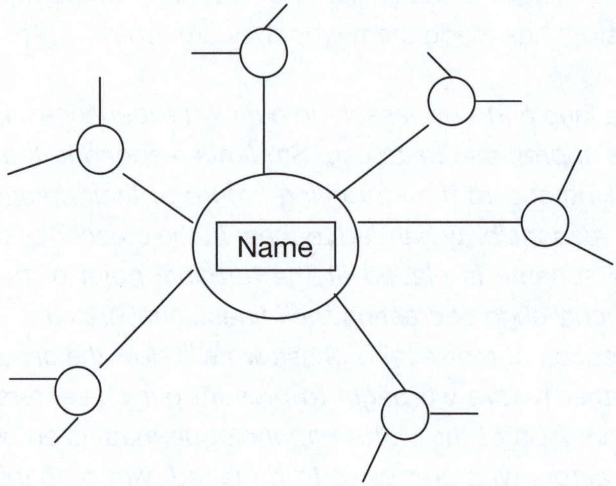

Figure 1

The name of another person.
A relationship.
A place.
A state of weather.
A day.
A period of time (day, month, year, etc.)
A colour.
A time of day.
A piece of music.
A special occasion.
The name of a feeling.
An object.
Another colour.
A job.
Another object.

We will come back to these things later... but note that they all belong to the world of your character... though perhaps in ways that we have not yet imagined.

13. *Now look again at the face. Stand. Place the picture in front of you on the floor. Take five steps away from your chair. Look away. I am going to give a signal now and at the signal you have to feel a 'snap' and a point of change at which you are going to stop being you and start being this other person. You should feel different. Your body should be doing different things. OK. Think about the character. How do they feel about being in the world? What is their name? WAIT. Clap. Go to your chair. Pick up your picture. Pick up the chair in character. Carry it to your place in the circle. Sit down. WAIT.*

Part Two: Sharing with the group

14. The group is now assembled. The teacher is now in role as the group's counsellor. You introduce yourself. I have always found it helpful to be an irritating and insensitive group-counsellor. You are slightly amused by the sad array of 'inadequates' before you. This has to be very subtle, but helps to cement the group by giving them something to oppose together. You can be slightly patronising but also quite authoritarian if challenged. You may use their first names too familiarly. The processes of the group drama are fairly simple:

● This is a self-help meeting for people who struggle to cope (a 'mental well-being' group, perhaps).
● Characters introduce themselves. Say why they are here at the meeting.
● Ask directed questions to establish the group. What makes you angry? Who has hurt you most?

Take people's comments and try to get others to add on to what has been said; to 'share'. 'That's very interesting . . . does this relate to anybody else?' The falseness of your character is important because it makes the whole situation a 'performance'. This isn't 'method'. This is exploration and creation.

After some time of building the group and letting the actors explore their characters in a social setting, raise the stakes . . .

15. *We are here to share. To be honest. I've a feeling some of us are not opening up . . . I know I'm paid by the hour . . . but please . . . we need to make progress . . . Before you came to the meeting you were asked to prepare what you wished to share with the group. You were asked to*

make notes... to help you to focus in a very emotional situation. Now it's time to share. If you have your notes (the word-map prepared earlier) please take it out now. Who wants to go first?

16. Now take it in turns to spotlight each character. Encourage them to use their notes. They each tell their story. Expect the pace to be slow and some students to need great support, including your close questioning. Other characters are invited to ask questions. This will take some time. The stories they create at this point will be the raw materials on which their final pieces of drama are based. Beginning in such a focused and serious atmosphere these narratives are likely to be highly developed even at this stage. The process here is one of making detailed, improvised monologues.

Part Three: Exploring a public encounter

At the end of 'story-telling' sessions we will move the characters into more public situations.

17. The characters have not been in a pub since the start of their 'troubles'. This may be many years. They have not felt able to deal with other adults in a public and unprotected situation. The group leader (your character) is going to set them a task. This is what you will say:

You are doing very well, friends. Everybody here has started on their journeys back out to the world. I am going to set you homework... yes, homework. Before you leave tonight I would like you all to make an arrangement to meet one evening before our next meeting. You will meet in a public house or bar that you all agree on. You must meet with one or two other people. Next week we may be asking you to report back on how things went. Look around the circle now and decide who you would like to know a little better. Who do you feel a special connection with?

Now go and stand with these people against the wall, or outside of this space. Please don't talk yet.

18. This might be a point at which to break with the drama, having anticipated later sessions. Or you might find yourself launching straight into the new scenario. In which case, continue. As the characters form groups and move to the edge of the space rearrange their chairs to approximate a pub. Establish a bar, with small tables if possible. You might play some music to suggest a juke box or a bar atmosphere sound effect.

19. Out of role explain: Here is the pub. Here is the bar. All the meetings are going to take place in the same space... but each group meeting has to accept that all the *other* groups of characters are strangers to you. Really, you're all meeting in different pubs. You will all enter at different times. Now all stand as if you are about to enter the pub. Before you do so stand and prepare. Take yourself to the edge of the space and stand facing outwards. Imagine yourself as your character looking into a mirror for the last time before leaving your room or house to go to the meeting. Adopt their posture and stance. Ask yourself:

- How do you feel?
- How do you feel about the people in this pub: the strangers?
- Why did you choose this pub?
- What do you think the strangers will think or say about you when you walk in?
- What drink will you order?
- Do you think the others will turn up?

20. Tell the group: The first person from each group can enter the pub when they feel ready. There is no hurry. The others will join in a few moments. To enter the pub you must walk through the door which is marked out by these two chairs. OK? You are on your own.

Begin the spontaneous improvisation. You will function as the bartender. As with your earlier character it may be useful to be mildly antagonistic and impatient with these people.

Let the characters interact. Let the actors settle into their roles.

Sooner or later characters will begin to leave the scene. When they do so, ask them to stand with their backs to the 'stage' and not watch.

At the end of the improvisation stop and make sure actors are out of character. Explain:

We are not going to watch the scenes that you have just improvised. What we are after is for you to feel 'absorbed' in the person you have created... but we also want you to *use* the character to create theatre. This work is all research for your final piece of drama. Think about the scene you have just imagined and acted. Think about it as a writer might. You wish to communicate your character to your audience; to give them an insight into this human being, who they are and how they live. In five minutes' time I want you to show us as much or as little of the scene as you think feels right. We want to see the moments of your scene that show your character at their most interesting. This should be a strong moment of theatre. It will be strong not because of 'action' or emotional momentum, but because of the joy of watching a well-painted character. If you can thrill us with just your presentation of character, we can say that you have **earned your actor's stripes!**

Students prepare the edited scenes.

Students perform their scenes.

21. Discuss with the group: Why did you choose to show these moments? What *is* a 'strong moment of theatre'? What do the moments you have chosen mean? This set of characters has a particular idea of what it is like to *be* in the world... what do they think? What do YOU think about what they think? How do you feel about the fact that you have created this person out of nothing? Your imagination 'gave' you this character? What does it mean to you as the actor? What does it mean to us as the audience? What do these characters and these scenes show us about human life and people? This is a move from the 'particular' example of your character, to the 'general' statement about human life. What idea do you wish to use your character to express?

Having created the characters from private acts of imagination, in this section we have put the characters to work in a social setting. To understand a person you not only have to understand their story or their physicality you also need to understand their place within the world and their attitude towards that social place.

As a part of this work students have also been introduced to Milos Forman's film adaptation of One flew over the cuckoo's nest. *In the film we see the development of a series of vulnerable individuals within a very particular social setting dominated by the formidable Nurse Ratchet. The film, one of the most accomplished pieces of American cinema, touches all bases for this scheme of work; fully realised character expressed physically and vocally, the importance and intrusion of life history into character and the subtlety of character-centred drama. As we move to the final phase of the scheme the narrative also demonstrates important aspects of dramatic structure: the status quo disturbed, the conflict of controlling characters and ideas, characters representing ideas, moments of reversal and the gathering storm of the dramatic, liberating peak.*

Phase 3: The hand-over

22. Explain to the group: What we have been doing for the past few lessons is exploring character. 'Building a character' is the root of what an actor does. At the same time we have been exploring the 'down-side' of what if feels like to be a vulnerable person in the world in which we live. We have said, 'A person struggles'. How do they struggle? What is their struggle with? Why do they struggle? Your character and their stories are the answers you have all given.

23. 'Now, all of our explorations have been leading us here. As I have said, we are about to begin to create our last ever piece of drama together. Even if something is telling you that it is not going to be your last . . . I want you to imagine that it is. The things you've always thought you were capable of doing in drama, the things you want to do, the way you want to be . . . Imagine that this is your last chance.

24. 'The characters, their situations and their stories are the raw materials on which you must now base your drama. From here on my input will be to help you develop your own theatre. From what we have done together I want you to understand the role of full characterisation in your dramas. The characters can be made to 'populate' each others' stories; maybe she's the sister you've told us about, maybe he's the father . . . You can develop, alter your characters. Whatever you end up telling us and whoever you end up playing in your dramas you must know as much about your character as you do now about this character. It seems that some of these characters belong together. What are those connections? The process of developing a narrative around these characters should be a natural one.

   Let us begin.

   What follows is a creative outburst. What results should be the strongest pieces of work your group has been engaged in. You have offered a rich pallet of character and narrative and now, you offer the group the gift of a blank canvas on which they can construct rich, dramatic texts of their own.

Afterword

We need to go public. If we are capable of such rich experience on a routine basis, people need to know: parents, colleagues, managers, officers, politicians. In the presence of the experience for which we work, no open person – no person with a genuine interest in the education of the young – could deny its force. We need an open door. We need to share that which we can. To find new ways to reveal what we *have* and what we *are*. When we are known, we are untouchable. Our strength is the experience. What we do matters. We change the world by touching lives with meaning. Drama is an intervention on nothingness. Drama seeks life.

Keep faith.

Be great.

A bell is ringing.

Have a good day.

Bibliography and further reading

The Collected Works of Dorothy Heathcote, Dorothy Heathcote, Cecily O'Neil and Liz Johnston (eds), 1991, Northwestern University Press.

Tuesday, Edward Bond, 1993, Methuen.

The Hidden Plot, Edward Bond, 1999, Methuen.

Brain-based Learning: The New Paradigm of Teaching, Eric Jensen, 2008, Corwin.

How the Brain Learns, David A. Souza, 2011, Corwin.

Frames of Mind: The Theory of Multiple Intelligences, Howard Gardner, 2011, Basic Books.

Emotional Intelligence: Why it Can Matter More Than IQ, Daniel Goleman, 1996, Bloomsbury.

Learning Through Drama: Report of the Schools Council Drama Teaching Project, Lynne McGregor, Maggie Tate, and Ken Robinson, Heinemann, 1977.

All Our Futures: Creativity, Culture and Education, Department of Education and Employment, (UK) 1999.

Out of Our Minds: Learning to be Creative, Ken Robinson, 2011, Capstone.

The Element: How Finding Your Passion Changes Everything, Ken Robinson and Lou Aronica, 2010, Penguin.

Structuring Drama Work, 2nd edition, Jonothan Neelands and Tony Goode, 2000, Cambridge University Press.

National Association for the Teaching of English Drama Pack: Basic, Ruth Moore and Paul Bunyan. NATE, available at: www.nate.org.uk/index.php?page=11&cat=8

By the same author and published by Routledge/David Fulton (addressed to primary school teachers, but also of interest to Drama specialists).

A Practical Guide to Shakespeare for the Primary School, John Doona, 2011, David Fulton/Routledge.

Drama Lessons for the Primary School Years, John Doona, 2012, David Fulton/Routledge.

Why Bond Matters, John Doona, NATD and National Drama, available at: www.johndoona.com/articles.html alongside other published articles.